THE AB GUIDE TO

The AB Guide to Music Theory

Part I

ERIC TAYLOR

The Associated Board of
the Royal Schools of Music

First published in 1989 by
the Associated Board of the Royal Schools of Music (Publishing) Ltd

Reprinted in 1990 (with revisions), 1991, 1992, 1993 (with revisions),
1994, 1995, 1996, 1997, 1998, 1999, 2000, 2002, 2003, 2004, 2005,
2006, 2007

© 1989 by The Associated Board of the Royal Schools of Music

ISBN 1 85472 446 0

Typesetting and music processing by
Halstan & Co. Ltd, Amersham, Bucks
Printed in England by
Page Bros Ltd, Norwich

CONTENTS

Chapter 7: Intervals and Transposition

Chapter 8: Triads and Chords

Chapter 9: Phrases and Cadences

Chapter 10: Tempo, Dynamics and Mood

Chapter 11: Articulation

Chapter 12: Ornaments and Embellishments

Chapter 13: Reiterations and Repeats

PREFACE

People sang and played instruments long before ways of writing music down on paper were invented. Even today, nearly everyone can sing, though not everyone can 'read' music. Many people can also play instruments without being able to read a note of music: like some of the great jazz musicians, they play 'by ear'.

Clearly, it is perfectly possible to make music without having it written down. Indeed, when one considers the world's music as a whole, one finds that the use of music **notation** (written signs representing musical sounds) is actually quite rare. Many countries in the East, for example, have ancient musical traditions which are very beautiful and sometimes very elaborate, yet which make little (if any) use of notation. Their musicians scarcely ever learn from written-down music or use it when they are performing.

In Europe, however, the use of notation became central to the development of music. At first (well over a thousand years ago) it amounted to nothing more than a few simple signs inserted in books containing the words of texts chanted in monasteries. These signs were only rough reminders: they helped the monks to recall music which they had learnt in the past but had not sung recently. Gradually the signs became more detailed, until they ceased to be mere reminders and became exact guides. Musicians were enabled to perform music straight from the notation: they no longer had to learn it by listening to someone else performing it first; they no longer had to memorise it. This development helped the spread of new music, for once a piece had been written down it could be performed by other musicians – perhaps living many miles away – even though they had never heard it. Even more important, the use of music notation opened the way to more and more complicated music. It became possible for a composer to work out how several singers or players could have independent parts which would nevertheless sound well together, and then to provide each of the performers with the appropriate notation.

These two factors – the dissemination of music through manuscript or printed copies, and the increasing complexity made possible by notation – produced over many centuries what might be called a shared European musical language. It is true that different countries or regions (Britain, France, Germany, Italy, Spain etc.) sometimes had special characteristics of their own, but these are relatively unimportant, like the local dialects which can be found in a spoken language. The European musical language passed to America and then spread to many other parts of the world, so that it has become cosmopolitan. Thus it is the common language not only of Bach, Mozart and Beethoven but also of many other composers of different nationalities and periods. It is also the common language of the Hollywood musical, jazz, rock and pop as well as of the piped music which has become inescapable in shops, offices, factories, hotels and other public places.

The notation of this musical language, and the terms used by musicians, are what this book is about. Such aspects of music are commonly referred to as 'theory'. The Associated Board of the Royal Schools of Music, for example, makes a distinction between 'Theory' and 'Practical' examinations: the former involving written papers, the latter being concerned with performance (either singing or playing an instrument). The distinction is convenient, but it can also be misleading. In ordinary speech, 'theory' is often used as the opposite of 'practice'. In the sense in which it is generally used in music, however, 'theory' is a thoroughly practical matter. Beethoven's symphonies would have stayed in his head and we should never had heard them if he had not been able to write them down on paper, and if performers did not understand exactly what his written signs meant. Nor could musicians rehearse together if they did not all know the meaning of terms such as 'F sharp', 'crescendo', '6/8', 'rallentando', 'Da Capo' and so on.

As with spoken language, musical language is always developing. We no longer express things in quite the same way that Shakespeare and his contemporaries would have done. Some words have changed their meaning slightly, others have fallen into disuse, while new words have been added to the language. There are even changes in the ways in which we write language down. Our spelling is more standardised than it was in Shakespeare's day, and our use of punctuation is slightly different. It is the same in music. Some musical signs which once were common are now rarely found; others have changed their meaning. New musical ideas have necessitated new developments in notation.

We often talk loosely about 'rules' in music, but really there are no rules, and never have been – not, at least, in the sense that somewhere there exists or has existed an official body of legislators decreeing what composers may or may not do. The so-called 'rules' are no more than *conventions* derived from a study of what composers have actually composed, how they have written their music down, and how it has been performed. At some periods these conventions have changed slowly, at others very rapidly. At no time, however, have they been completely static, and it can never be assumed that the conventions which we now take for granted apply equally to the music of past ages.

This is particularly important in the matter of notation. The notation which will be used and explained in the following pages is the notation generally used today, with the meaning it has for today's musicians. But some older conventions will be mentioned too, for although modern composers may not observe them, they are important in earlier music which is still regularly performed.

The AB Guide to Music Theory, then, is an attempt to help people learning music to understand how it is written down, what the various signs and symbols denote, and what the common technical words used by musicians mean. These, of course, are not matters which are merely of concern to students preparing for theory examinations: they are vital to *all* musicians, including performers and those who wish to write their own music. Nevertheless they are the specific subject of theory examinations, and *The AB Guide* therefore includes the basic information required in the Associated Board's Theory examinations.

Broadly speaking, Part I deals with the subjects which arise in Grades 1 to 5, Part II with those which occur in the higher grades. The information has not been broken up to correspond with the individual grades since this would result in too disrupted an account of many topics. A grade-by-grade approach is, however, adopted in the Associated Board's series of booklets called *Music Theory in Practice*, and a student preparing for an Associated Board Theory examination should certainly start with the booklet for the appropriate grade. In it will be found a detailed list of the requirements of the particular grade, references to sections of the present book where the relevant information is to be found, supplementary information which may be needed in the context of the examination, and specimen questions and exercises – together with guidance on their solutions.

Finally, I wish to record my deep gratitude to a number of people who have read this book, or part of it, at various stages in its preparation: Professor Peter Aston, Dr Peter Le Huray, Dr H. Diack Johnstone, Dr Richard Jones, Mr Desmond Ratcliffe, Professor Raymond Warren, and Mr Percy Welton. Without their advice, many faults might, I fear, have remained undetected, many gaps unfilled, and many ambiguities unclarified. Since, however, none of them has read the book in its entirety in its final form (and also, it has to be admitted, since I have not invariably adopted their suggestions) they are not to be blamed for any errors which it may yet contain, or for anything with which they would disagree.

Goring Heath, 1989   ERIC TAYLOR

ACKNOWLEDGEMENTS

Thanks are due to the following publishers for permission to reproduce passages from copyright music:

Boosey & Hawkes Music Publishers Ltd, London
    Bartók, *Concerto for Orchestra*
    Bartók, *For Children*
    Leonard Bernstein & Stephen Sondheim, 'Maria' (*West Side Story*)
    Britten, *Serenade for Tenor, Horn & Strings*
    Ireland, *Holy Boy*
    Prokofiev, *Classical Symphony*
    Stravinsky, *Petrouchka*

Breitkopf & Härtel, Wiesbaden
    Sibelius, Symphony No.1

Oxford University Press, Oxford
    Vaughan Williams, *The Lark Ascending*
    Walton, *Belshazzar's Feast*

PART I

CHAPTER 1

The Basics of Rhythm and Tempo

1/1 Time values

When soldiers march along behind a band, their footsteps are absolutely regular and even. The music helps to keep them together: more likely than not, in fact, the big drum will be struck together with every footstep. We say that the music has a steady beat or pulse, and that the soldiers are marching in time to the music.

The sign most often used for a single beat is ♩ and it is called a **crotchet**. Thus the regular sound of the soldiers' marching feet – left, right, left, right – can be shown in music notation like this – ♩♩♩♩ .

If the big drum were to be struck with every footstep, its sounds would be written in the same way – ♩♩♩♩ . But if it were to be struck only with every *second* footstep (e.g. with every left foot), a different sign would be needed. The sign used is ♩ and it is called a **minim**. The signs for the soldiers' footsteps (crotchets) and the strokes on the big drum (minims) could be lined up together –

big drum   ♩   ♩

footsteps   ♩   ♩   ♩   ♩
                (left, right, left, right)

Clearly, one minim lasts as long as two crotchets.

A small drum in the band might be played with more drum-strokes: for example, two equal strokes to every footstep. In that case, each drum-stroke would be shown by a sign called a **quaver**, ♪, and the footsteps, big drum and small drum could all be lined up together thus –

big drum   ♩   ♩

footsteps   ♩   ♩   ♩   ♩

small drum   ♪ ♪ ♪ ♪ ♪ ♪ ♪ ♪

A minim, therefore, can be divided into two crotchets or four quavers.

Longer and shorter sounds can also be written. A **semibreve**, o, is twice as long as a minim, but a **semiquaver**, ♪, lasts only half as long as a quaver.

Signs like these, which are used to represent musical sounds, are called notes[1]. The design of a note shows its 'value' – how long it lasts. Thus semibreves, minims etc. may be described as **time values** or **note values**.

The words 'semibreve', 'minim', 'crotchet' etc. are the ones commonly used in Britain and in some other English-speaking countries. But in others, including the U.S.A., the following terms are preferred: 'whole', 'half', 'quarter', 'eighth' and 'sixteenth' notes. It is easy to see why from this table, in which each line lasts exactly the same time –

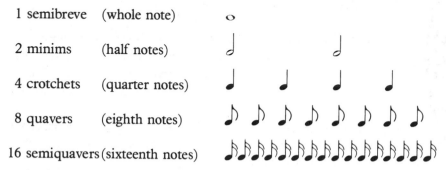

1 semibreve   (whole note)

2 minims   (half notes)

4 crotchets   (quarter notes)

8 quavers   (eighth notes)

16 semiquavers (sixteenth notes)

As the word 'semibreve' suggests, there is a sound which lasts twice as long called a **breve**. It is usually shown as ⊏o⊐ or ⊩o⊪, though an older form, ⊟, may also be found.

Although the breve is rarely used nowadays, very short notes are more common. Only half the length of a semiquaver is the **demisemiquaver**, ♪, 32 of which last as long as a semibreve. Even shorter notes may be found, e.g. the hemidemisemiquaver or sixty-fourth note, ♪.

Two or more quavers or shorter notes can be joined together –

♪♪   can be written as   ♫

♪♪   can be written as   ♫

♪♪♪♪   can be written as   ♫♫

♪♪♪♪   can be written as   ♫♫

[1]Like some other words in music, 'note' has several meanings. It can refer to a sound as well as to a written sign (e.g. a singer may ask for 'the note' before starting to sing), and it can also be used to describe 'notes' on a keyboard. In some countries the word 'tone' is used to mean a sound and not a written sign, but 'tone' is another word with more than one meaning, as will be seen in Chapter 2.

Mixed groups can also be joined together –

♪ ♪♪ can be written as

♪♪♪ can be written as

♪♪ ♪ can be written as

(More will be said about these groupings in 5/1.)

The names of the various parts of the written signs or notes are as follows –

♪ = ● + | +)

    note-head   stem   tail (or flag)

♫ = ●● + || + ▬

    note-heads   stems   beam

Groups of notes joined by a **beam** are said to be 'beamed' together.

As will be explained in Chapter 2, a stem may go either up or down from the note-head. If it goes up, it is placed on the right ♩ ♩ ♪♫ etc.; and if it goes down, it is placed on the left etc.; but note that a tail is always positioned on the right. This is the standard practice in printed music today. However, composers sometimes put the down-stems on the right (etc.) because it is quicker to write them that way; but this is not to be encouraged, and no one should ever write .

1/2 Time signatures

The sound of the soldiers' marching feet is an example of a succession of equal beats. Although the beats all last the same time, it is usual to think of them in groups, with some beats stronger than others. Marching feet, for example, naturally make groups of two beats –

LEFT right, LEFT right.

In music notation these groups are separated by vertical lines called **bar-lines**,

♩ ♩ | ♩ ♩ | ♩ ♩ | .

One group like this is called a **bar** (or 'measure' in some countries).

At the beginning of a piece of music there is a sign called a **time signature**. The time signature for the marching feet above would be $\frac{2}{4}$. This means that there are two crotchets in every bar – or notes which together last as long as two crotchets, e.g. –

$\frac{2}{4}$ ♩ ♩ | ♩ ♫ | ♫♫ | ♩ |

If the time signature were ¾, it would mean that there are three crotchets (or their equivalent) in every bar –

Clearly the top figure in the time signature shows *how many* beats there are in a bar.

The meaning of the bottom figure in a time signature is not quite so straightforward. So far in this chapter the crotchet has always been used as the sign for a single beat; but composers sometimes use a minim or a quaver instead (or even a semibreve or a semiquaver, although these are rare). If the minim is used as the sign for one beat, a crotchet will therefore represent only half a beat. Similarly, if a quaver is used as the sign for one beat, a crotchet will represent two beats.

The bottom figure in the time signature shows what *kind* of note is to be used to represent the beat. If the bottom figure is 4, the beats will be shown as crotchets; if it is 2, the beats will be minims; if it is 8, they will be quavers. (It is helpful here to remember the alternative word for minims, crotchets etc.: half notes, quarter notes etc.) Thus the time signature ⅜ means that there are three beats in every bar and that the beats are written as quavers –

Here are some further illustrations –

The first beat of the bar is the strongest, e.g. –

    strong   weak   weak   strong   weak   weak

This does not imply that in performance first beats have to be hammered! – nor, as will be seen in 6/3, that composers never depart from the basic pattern of strong and weak beats in a piece.

In practice, it is usual to think of beats as being grouped in twos or threes. Consequently, a bar of four is divided into two groups of twos –

    strong   weak   strong   weak

though with the third beat rather less strong than the first. Similarly, a bar of five beats will usually be heard as 3 + 2 or 2 + 3 (see also 5/3). This tendency to arrange equal beats into patterns of strong and weak beats extends also to subdivisions of beats. In $\frac{2}{4}$ ♪♪♪♪ |, for example, the second and fourth quavers are felt to be weaker than the first and third.

Time signatures were not always written in figures: they were formerly expressed by symbols such as circles and half-circles, sometimes crossed with a vertical line. Most of these symbols had disappeared by the early 17th century, but two survived well into the 20th century, though in a modified form: **C** and **¢** . **C** has exactly the same meaning as $\frac{4}{4}$, known as 'common time'. **¢** nowadays means the same as $\frac{2}{2}$, often called **alla breve** (although earlier in the history of music both **¢** and *alla breve* could also indicate what is now $\frac{4}{2}$).

If the 'time' ($\frac{2}{4}$, $\frac{3}{8}$ etc.) of a piece is unchanged throughout, the time signature is written at the beginning *only*. But it can change during a piece, even from bar to bar, and that change must be shown by a new time signature. This then remains in force until the end of the piece or until another time signature appears, e.g. –

$\frac{2}{4}$ ♩ ♪♪♪ | $\frac{3}{8}$ ♩ ♪ ♪♪♪ | $\frac{2}{4}$ ♩ ♩ | $\frac{3}{4}$ ♩ ♪♪♪ | ♩ ♩ |

At the end of a piece of music, a **double bar-line** is ruled, a thin one followed by a thick one –

$\frac{4}{4}$ ♪♪♪♪ ♩ ♩ | o ‖

Thin double bar-lines are used to mark the end of a principal section in a piece.

1/3 Tempo

The time signature indicates how many beats there are in a bar and the kind of note (crotchet, minim etc.) being used to represent a beat. What the time signature does not show is just *how fast* the beats are moving. A piece in $\frac{2}{4}$ or $\frac{4}{4}$ could be a march: but is it a quick march or a funeral march? The speed of the beats is called the **tempo**: a funeral march, for instance, would be said to be 'in a slow tempo'.

Expressions like 'slow tempo' or 'quick tempo' are somewhat vague, but composers can indicate exactly the speed they want. To do this they use a device called a **metronome** or 'Maelzel's metronome' (named after the man who patented the invention in 1815). It makes a steady, ticking sound – like a clock, except that it can be adjusted to tick at any speed one wishes. (Other types are now available, including electronic versions with a flashing light.) The metronome can be set to tick (or flash) at a given number of beats in a minute, and this number may be shown at the start of the music, thus: ♩ = 60 or M.M. ♩ = 60, (M.M. being an abbreviation for Maelzel's metronome). This means that there are 60 crotchet beats in a minute (i.e. one a second, which can easily be checked against a clock or watch). Similarly, ♪ = 48 means 48 quaver beats in a minute, ♩ = 100 means 100 minim beats in a minute, and so on. Thus, the following two examples would sound exactly the same and last just as long –

Before the invention of the metronome, composers could show the speed they wanted only approximately, by writing such words as 'slow', 'moderate' or 'quick'. Even today many prefer to use words rather than to give an exact speed by means of a metronome figure (or 'metronome mark' as it is usually called). In earlier days the words were generally written in Italian – and often still are – although other languages (e.g. German, English or French) are now frequently used instead. The most common foreign words are listed in the Glossary of Foreign Words used for Performance Directions. More will be said about tempo in 10/1.

1/4 Rhythm

This chapter is headed 'The Basics of Rhythm and Tempo'. The two are not the same. 'Rhythm' refers to the way in which sounds of varying length and accentuation are grouped into patterns. One way to understand it is to think of a familiar tune – say a song or a march: although the tune itself could not be played on a table, its rhythm could be tapped out on one. If it were to be tapped out more quickly or more slowly, its rhythm would not change: only its tempo.

CHAPTER 2

Introduction to Pitch

2/1 Pitch names and notation

Playing any note on a piano produces a fixed sound. The sound gradually fades away, but it does not go up or down. Music is made up from fixed sounds such as this.

Many instruments (including all the stringed instruments and the trombone) are capable of producing an infinite number of fixed sounds between any two notes on a keyboard, with only minute differences between them. It is the same with the human voice. But in practice all instruments, and singing voices too, normally use only the particular notes of the keyboard. When a player such as a violinist 'tunes' his instrument, he is trying to find *exactly* the one fixed sound he wants. All the other notes in the music will be placed in relation to this one note.

If one note is played on the keyboard and then another note is played anywhere to the right of it, the sound of the second note is said to be higher than that of the first. A note to the left of it would produce a lower sound. In the same way men's voices are said to be lower than those of women or young boys. The technical word referring to the height or depth of sound is **pitch**.

On the keyboard, groups of two black notes alternate with groups of three black notes. This makes it easy to distinguish between the white notes, which are given the letter names from A to G. A is always between the second and third of the group of three black notes. After G comes A again.

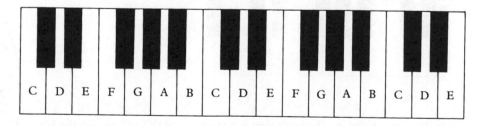

Keyboard players usually take their bearings from **middle C**: the C nearest to the centre of the keyboard. To orchestral players the A above middle C is more important, because this is the note to which they tune their instruments. The distance from any note to the next one with the same letter name (e.g. from A to A or B to B) is an **octave**: eight notes in all.

The familiar five lines on which music is written are known as the **stave** or **staff** –

The lines and spaces between them are counted from the bottom –

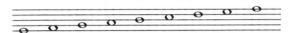

fifth line
fourth space
fourth line
third space
third line
second space
second line
first space
first line

Each line and each space represent a note, so there are nine notes here –

But *which* nine? To answer this question, a sign called a **clef** is always placed at the beginning of every stave. There are several different clefs, but the most common one is 𝄞 and is called the **treble clef**. It is also known as the 'G' clef, because the middle part of it ⟨ is always looped around a line ⟨, and that line represents the G above middle C. Today the treble clef is always looped around the second line (but see Appendix E in Part II for another position which has been used in the past). In consequence, a note placed on that line will be the G above middle C, and all the other notes on the stave can be related to the notes on the keyboard too –

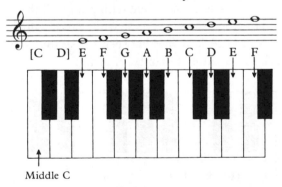

[C D] E F G A B C D E F

Middle C

For the lower notes on the keyboard a different clef has to be used: the **bass clef** or 'F' clef, which can be shown in either of two ways: 𝄢 or 𝄢. In both cases the two dots are written either side of a line and that line then represents the F below middle C. Nowadays the clef is always placed on the 4th line – 𝄢 or 𝄢, although, as with the G clef, other positions have been used in the past (see Appendix E in Part II).

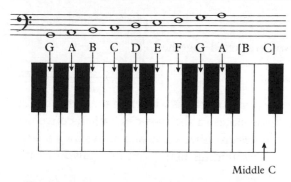

Middle C

The stem of a note on the middle line of a stave may go either up or down – ![up-stem] or ![down-stem] – but normally stems of lower notes go up and those of higher notes go down – ![example] . (See 3/1 for exceptions.)

To provide for notes which lie above or below the limits of the stave, short additional lines called **ledger lines** (or leger lines) are used. Each note above or below the stave has its own line or lines: they are not joined together –

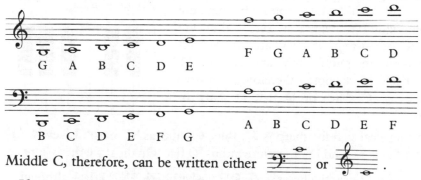

Middle C, therefore, can be written either ![bass clef middle C] or ![treble clef middle C] .

If necessary, further ledger lines may be used for higher or lower notes. However, to avoid many ledger lines, the sign **8** or **8va** (= *ottava*, Italian for 'octave') can be used above or below notes, indicating that they are to be played an octave higher or lower. It is placed by the first note to which it refers and is followed by a continuous line (or a dotted line), with ⌐ or ⌐ at the end to show where the *8va* direction finishes –

Piano music uses two staves bracketed together:

Usually the top stave is for the right-hand notes written in the treble clef and the bottom stave for the left-hand notes in the bass clef. When convenient, however, both hands may play notes on either stave, and both staves may use either clef. Middle C (and its surrounding notes) can be shown on either stave –

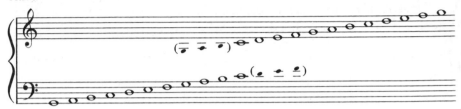

Black notes on the keyboard take their names from the white notes. If they are to the right (i.e. higher in pitch) they are said to be **sharp**; if they are to the left (i.e. lower in pitch) they are said to be **flat**. Each black note, therefore, has two names, e.g. C sharp or D flat, D sharp or E flat.

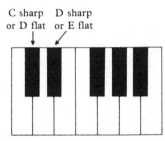

The musical sign for sharp is ♯ : thus C♯ means 'C sharp'. Likewise, the sign for flat is ♭, and D♭ therefore means 'D flat'. On the stave these signs are always placed *before* the notes – C sharp, D flat – although in ordinary writing they come afterwards – C♯, D♭ etc.

To return to the original white note after it has been made sharp or flat, a **natural** sign, ♮, is used –

The distance in pitch (or **interval**) between any note and its nearest neighbour, black or white, is called a **semitone** (half tone). Thus, the interval between C and C♯ or between C♯ and D is a semitone, and so also is the interval between E and F. An interval of two semitones, e.g. C to D or C to B♭, is described as an interval of a **tone** –

Because the ♯ sign always raises a note a semitone and the ♭ sign always lowers it a semitone, white notes on the keyboard can also be written and named in different ways. For example –

When two notes have the same sound but different names, they are called **enharmonics**. C♯ is the enharmonic of D♭, and vice versa. But although a note may be 'spelt' in two different ways, it is not generally the case that either spelling may be used: usually one is correct and the other wrong. One factor which may decide the choice is the scale (to be explained shortly) on which the music is based.

2/2 The major scale

Virtually all pieces of music written before the early 20th century do not use *all* the black and white notes but only a selection of them. When they are arranged in ascending or descending order, the particular notes of a piece are called a **scale** (the word originally meant a 'ladder'). The most common scale of all can be found by playing just the white notes on the keyboard from any C to the next C above or below –

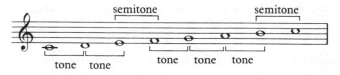

These notes, which can be compared to the rungs on a ladder, are described as **degrees** of the scale: the first (i.e. the lowest) is the 'first degree', and so on as shown in the example above.

It can be seen that this scale consists of a mixture of tones and semitones –

This particular series – tone, tone, semitone, tone, tone, tone, semitone (or T T S T T T S for short) – is called a **major scale**. Since the scale above starts on C, it is known as the 'scale of C major'. *Any* note can be used as the first note of a major scale; but if the scale starts on any note except C, one or

more of the black notes will have to be used in order to preserve the series
T T S T T T S. If it starts on G, for example, an F *sharp* will be needed –

The F♯ cannot be written as G♭, its enharmonic, because one of the rungs
of the ladder would then be missing: there
would be no F of any kind.

    Similarly, if the scale starts on F, a B *flat* will be needed –

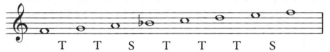

while a start on D would need *two* sharps (F♯ and C♯) –

The three scales above are those of G major, F major and D major
respectively. A piece of music which uses the notes of the scale of G major, for
instance, is said to be in the **key** of G major or just 'in G major'. The note on
which a scale begins (i.e. the first degree) is the **key-note**.

2/3 Key signatures

To say that a piece of music is based on the notes of the scale of C major does
not mean that it is restricted to eight notes. The eight notes of the basic scale
can be used at any pitch, one or more octaves higher or lower. But except for
special purposes the notes of the basic scale will not be altered; thus, if a piece
is in G major, *all* the Fs will be F♯s. Similarly, *all* the Bs in a piece in F major
will be B♭s. It is not necessary to write in the sharps or flats every time they are
needed. Instead they are shown at the beginning of the piece, immediately

after the clef and before the time signature – . The sharp on the F line

is enough to show that all the Fs will be F♯s, not just those on the fifth line;
there is no need to put a sharp in the first space as well. In the bass clef it is

written – .

    This direction about the sharps and flats to be used is called the **key
signature**. The examples above show the key signature of G major. Here is

the key signature for D major as it appears at the start of a piano piece –

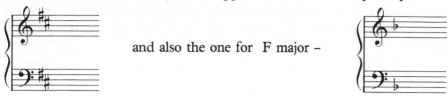

and also the one for F major –

Unlike the time signature (see 1/2), the key signature is repeated at the beginning of every line. If it has to be changed during the course of a piece, all that is needed is to write the new key signature after a double bar-line –

It used to be the practice to cancel the old key signature first with naturals – but nowadays naturals are only used when no sharps or flats follow –

A clef may be changed at any point in a line of music, but when it occurs between bars it is placed *before* the bar-line. (The key signature is not repeated.) Changes of time signature always come *after* the bar-line. The following example illustrates these conventions –

All changes of clef, time signature and key signature, which apply to the start of a *new* line, should also be shown at the end of the previous line –

2/4 Accidentals

During the course of a piece of music other sharps or flats, not included in the key signature, may sometimes be added to individual notes. Further, a sharp or a flat in the key signature may be cancelled by the use of a ♮. Sharps, flats and naturals used in this way are called **accidentals**. If an accidental appears only occasionally, it is unlikely to make any alteration to the key; but if it is used more frequently, it could involve a change of key, although it may not be necessary to write a new key signature.

Once an accidental has appeared in a bar, it remains in force until the end of the bar, hence –

NOT

If a note with an accidental is tied over a bar-line, the accidental is not written again –  . But if it were to be used again in the second bar, its next appearance would have to be marked –

Unlike the sharps and flats in a key signature, an accidental applies only to the line or space on which it is written. Thus, the second ♮ in the following example is needed –

The final B in the above example is a B♭. Some composers might put a ♭ before it (perhaps in brackets or in a small size) as a reminder, but this is not strictly necessary.

CHAPTER 3

Continuing with Rhythm

3/1 Rests

Music does not consist only of sounds: it includes silences too. Notation has to show how long each silence lasts, just as it shows how long each sound lasts. The signs used for silences are called **rests**.

A silence lasting as long as a crotchet is indicated by a crotchet rest, ⸿ (sometimes it is written ⌐ instead, but this sign is no longer standard). The sign for a quaver rest is ⅄ and the semiquaver rest is ⅄.

The minim and semibreve rests are attached to one of the lines of the stave. The minim rest sits on top of a line ▬, usually the third line – ▆ , while the semibreve rest hangs below a line, usually the fourth line – ▆ .

The breve rest completely fills the space between two lines – ▆ .

Here is a complete list of the rests corresponding to the notes already discussed –

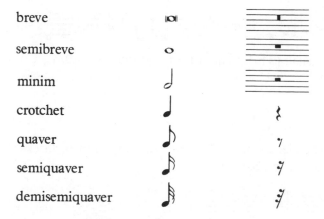

breve	𝄩	
semibreve	o	
minim	♩	
crotchet	♩	⸿
quaver	♪	⅄
semiquaver	♬	⅄
demisemiquaver	♬	⅄

An entirely silent bar in ⅔ time is shown by a breve rest, but an entirely silent bar in ¼ , and in every other time signature, is shown by a semibreve rest –

etc.

Sometimes two (or more) melodies are written on one stave. The rests may then have to be placed higher or lower than usual. For example, these two melodies –

may be combined on one stave –

When two melodies are combined in this way, the stems of the notes in the upper melody always go up and those in the lower melody go down. If the two melodies share the same note, it will be written with *two* stems, one up and one down, like the final note in the first bar of the above example. Two semibreves on the same note are made to overlap, as in the last bar. (Another way of writing them is to put them side by side, but touching, ∞.)

A piece of music may start on any beat of the bar, not just the first beat. If it starts after the first beat, the opening can be shown with or without preliminary rests –

Carol, 'God rest ye merry gentlemen'

though without is more usual. (This point is further discussed in 9/1.)

3/2 Ties and dots

Bar-lines make the music easier to read, but they also have some drawbacks. In this passage there is a missing bar-line –

but the bar-line is clearly needed in the *middle* of a note: the minim on the top note (F). However, bar-lines are never drawn through notes, only between them, so the passage has to be written like this –

The minim has been replaced by two crotchets with the bar-line between them, and the two crotchets are joined together by a curved line called a **tie**. Ties always start and finish at the *head* of a note, not the stem –

so if the stems go up, the tie will be below the notes –

However, when two ties are used simultaneously, they are written thus –

There is no limit to the number of notes which can be tied together. Although there are six *written* notes in the next example, there are only two *sounds*, the first of which lasts for the length of 18 crotchet beats –

Ties are used within bars as well as across bar-lines –

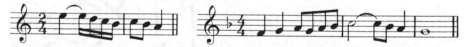

The first example starts with a sound (E in the treble clef) lasting for $1\frac{1}{4}$ crotchet beats. In the second example, the top note (C) lasts for $2\frac{1}{2}$ crotchet beats.

Ties are not the only way of lengthening notes. A note can be made half as long again by placing a **dot** after the note-head –

and rests can be dotted too –

but they are never tied: there would be no point!

Dots are not used to lengthen notes or rests across bar-lines. Consequently the tied A in this example cannot be replaced by a dotted note –

; and the two rests in the following example cannot be replaced by a dotted crotchet rest – .

A note or a rest may be followed by two dots: then it is said to be **double-dotted**[1]. The second dot adds half the length of the first dot –

𝅗𝅥.. is the same as 𝅗𝅥 𝅘𝅥 𝅘𝅥𝅮 and 𝄽·· is the same as 𝄽 𝄾 𝄿

3/3 Triplets and compound time

As mentioned in Chapter 1, a beat of any kind (crotchet, minim etc.) can be divided into two equal parts. The first bar of the following passage contains three crotchet beats each divided into two quavers –

attrib. J. S. Bach
Anna Magdalena Bach Notebook

A beat can also be divided into three equal parts, called a **triplet**. To indicate a triplet, a figure *3* is centred over or under the three notes –

and sometimes a curved line or square bracket is added –

The essential point is that, when a crotchet is divided into a triplet, the three notes are written as quavers, with a *3* to distinguish them from ordinary quavers. In other words, 𝅘𝅥 can be divided into 𝅘𝅥𝅮𝅘𝅥𝅮 or into 𝅘𝅥𝅮𝅘𝅥𝅮𝅘𝅥𝅮.

Any note can be divided into a triplet in the same way –

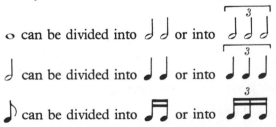

A triplet, then, is a group of three equal notes performed in the time normally taken by two notes of the same kind. Strictly speaking, one should

---

[1]Double dots were not used until the middle of the 18th century. Until then (and sometimes even later), notes with single dots were in some circumstances played as though they were double-dotted – or in other ways.

say 'three notes *or their equivalent*': all of these examples are triplet groups, and each takes the time of one crotchet to perform –

In a passage of continuous triplets, the *3*s are often omitted once the pattern has been established; and where triplets are obvious without *3*s, composers occasionally do not include a *3* at all.

In some pieces the beat *regularly* divides into threes, not twos, e.g. –

Sousa, March, 'The Liberty Bell'

This, however, is not the notation which Sousa actually used, because there is an easier method: one which avoids having to add *3*s throughout. What he actually wrote (and it sounds exactly the same) was –

The $\frac{2}{4}$ time signature has been changed to $\frac{6}{8}$, meaning six quavers (or their equivalent) in a bar. $\frac{6}{8}$ still implies *two* beats in a bar (like $\frac{2}{4}$), but the beats are now *dotted* crotchets. Notice that a dot has been added to the first note in the last bar to make it a full beat in $\frac{6}{8}$.

Both $\frac{3}{4}$ and $\frac{6}{8}$ have six quavers in a bar, but they are not the same thing. $\frac{3}{4}$ means *three* beats (crotchets) divided into twos; $\frac{6}{8}$ means *two* beats (dotted crotchets) divided into threes. The difference can be grasped by saying aloud –

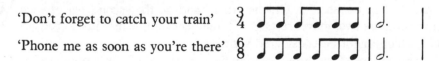

'Don't forget to catch your train'

'Phone me as soon as you're there'

When the beats divide into twos, the music is said to be in **simple time**; when they divide into threes, it is in **compound time**. For every simple time signature there is an equivalent compound time signature –

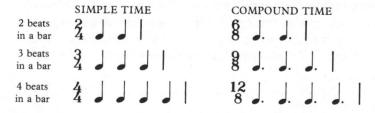

	SIMPLE TIME	COMPOUND TIME
2 beats in a bar	$\frac{2}{4}$ ♩ ♩	$\frac{6}{8}$ ♩. ♩.
3 beats in a bar	$\frac{3}{4}$ ♩ ♩ ♩	$\frac{9}{8}$ ♩. ♩. ♩.
4 beats in a bar	$\frac{4}{4}$ ♩ ♩ ♩ ♩	$\frac{12}{8}$ ♩. ♩. ♩. ♩.

Other words sometimes used are **duple, triple** and **quadruple**, meaning two, three or four beats (either simple or compound) in a bar. (Similarly, though much less common, **quintuple** means five beats in a bar and **septuple** seven beats in a bar.) Consequently –

$\frac{2}{4}$ is simple duple time $\frac{6}{8}$ is compound duple time

$\frac{3}{4}$ is simple triple time $\frac{9}{8}$ is compound triple time

$\frac{4}{4}$ is simple quadruple time $\frac{12}{8}$ is compound quadruple time

(Further examples of simple and compound time are given in 5/3).

3/4 The basis of simple and compound time notation

The difference between simple and compound time is made clear in the notation. On p.19, for example, the quavers corresponding to 'Don't forget to catch your train' were beamed together in twos, but those corresponding to 'Phone me as soon as you're there' were beamed in threes. Similarly, the lengths of the sounds and silences in these examples are exactly the same –

yet the signs used are not always the same. For instance, the ♩ in the last bar of the first example is written as ♪· ♪ in the second, and the ⅞ in the first becomes ↱ ↱ in the second. On the other hand, in the second bar of each example there are two quaver rests (↱ ↱): neither example uses just a crotchet rest(⅞), which might be considered simpler.

The conventions of rhythmic notation have changed little for more than 300 years. They have two aims: (i) to suggest the underlying pattern of beats, strong and weak (such as the three ♩ beats per bar in the first example above and the two ♩· beats per bar in the second); (ii) to make the music easier to read by using no more signs than are necessary to make the beats clear. A detailed explanation of how these aims are achieved will be given in Chapter 5. In later chapters it will be seen that composers occasionally depart from the standard notation for special reasons: e.g. to indicate a disturbance in the normal flow of the rhythm or to suggest the phrasing required – see 6/3 and 11/2.

CHAPTER 4

More Scales, Keys and Clefs

4/1 Major scales and the circle of fifths

In Chapter 2 we saw how the major scales starting on C, G, D and F were constructed. Here are some more major scales:

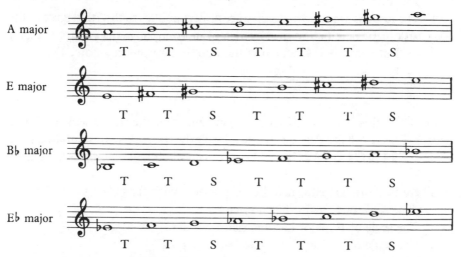

The key signatures of these scales are written thus –

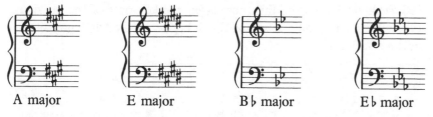

It will be noticed that no key signature has been made up of a mixture of sharps and flats: they have all included *either* sharps *or* flats. (As will be seen later, this is also true of all other key signatures.) If we concentrate first on key signatures with sharps, a pattern begins to emerge:

    (The scale of C major has no sharps)
    The scale of G major has one sharp: F♯
    The scale of D major has two sharps: F♯ C♯
    The scale of A major has three sharps: F♯ C♯ G♯
    The scale of E major has four sharps: F♯ C♯ G♯ D♯

From this pattern some important conclusions can be drawn:

(i)   Each scale begins on the 5th degree of the previous scale –

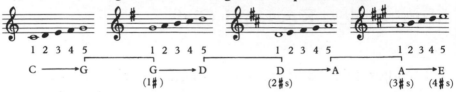

| 1 2 3 4 5 | 1 2 3 4 5 | 1 2 3 4 5 | 1 2 3 4 5 |

C ──→ G   G ──→ D   D ──→ A   A ──→ E
                   (1♯)   (2♯s)   (3♯s)   (4♯s)

(ii) Each scale adds one more sharp to those already in the previous scale.

(iii) The additional sharp is always five notes *above* the last sharp of the previous key signature.

(iv) The last sharp in the key signature always applies to the 7th degree of the scale – the note before the key-note. For example, in the scale of D major the last sharp is C♯, which is the note before the key-note, D –

1 2 3 4 5 6 7 8(= 1)

From all of this it is not difficult to work out that the major scale with five sharps (F♯ C♯ G♯ D♯ A♯) is B major. Similarly, the scale with six sharps is F♯ major (F♯ C♯ G♯ D♯ A♯ E♯). (The layouts of their key signatures are shown on p.27.)

There is a similar pattern in key signatures with flats –

(The scale of C major has no flats)
The scale of F major has one flat: B♭
The scale of B♭ major has two flats: B♭ E♭
The scale of E♭ major has three flats: B♭ E♭ A♭

Again we can draw some important conclusions:

(i)   Each scale begins on the fifth note *below* the key-note of the previous scale (which is the same as saying that it begins on the 4th degree of the previous scale) –

| 8 7 6 5 4 | 8 7 6 5 4 | 8 7 6 5 4 |

C ──→ F   F ──→ B♭   B♭ ──→ E♭
                   (1♭)   (2♭s)   (3♭s)

(ii) Each scale adds one more flat to those already in the previous scale.

(iii) The additional flat is always five notes *below* the last flat of the previous key signature.

(iv) The last flat is always the 4th degree of the scale. For example, in the scale of B♭ major the last flat is E♭ –

1 2 3 4 5 6 7 8(= 1)

It can now be deduced that the major scale with four flats is A♭ major (B♭ E♭ A♭ D♭), that the one with five flats is D♭ major (B♭ E♭ A♭ D♭ G♭), and that the one with six flats is G♭ major (B♭ E♭ A♭ D♭ G♭ C♭). (The layouts of these key signatures are shown on p.27.)

G♭, however, is the enharmonic of F♯, and F♯ (as already seen) is the key-note of the scale with six sharps. We seem to have come to a halt: we now have a major key signature for each note on the keyboard, indeed two for one of them (F♯/G♭). But if we were to carry on further, we would continue to get enharmonic alternatives. For example, if we extend the sequence of keys with sharp key signatures (G, D, A etc.) we get –

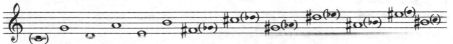

Now we *have* come to a halt, for we have ended up (enharmonically at least) where we started[1] – on C. Moreover, if we *reverse* this sequence and use the enharmonics (C F B♭ etc.), we find that it is just the same as the sequence of flat keys –

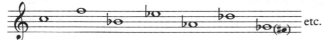

etc.

This can be shown more clearly as a circle, like a clock. If you read it clockwise you get the sequence of sharp keys, each with one sharp more than the previous one, i.e. five notes higher. Hence the sequence is known as the **circle of fifths**. If you read it anticlockwise you get the sequence of flat keys.

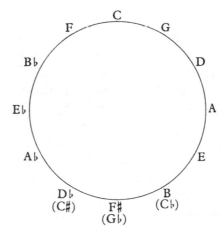

For various reasons, composers do sometimes go further than F♯ or G♭ major, e.g. by writing in C♯ major (seven sharps) rather than D♭ (five flats), or in C♭ major (seven flats) rather than B major (five sharps), but they usually choose the simpler alternative.

---

[1] If the laws of physics are strictly followed, this is not quite true: B♯ is not *quite* the same as C♮, nor are the earlier enharmonics exactly the same. To explain why this is so would take us into the study of acoustics and beyond the scope of this book; but it is worth noting that a tuner has to make very slight compromises to ensure that each note on a keyboard will be acceptable whatever function it has to serve (e.g. as F♯ or G♭) – a system called 'equal temperament'.

4/2 Minor scales and keys

After major scales, the next most common are **minor scales**. The special characteristics of music written in minor keys result in two types of minor scale, one of which is not the same ascending and descending.

The easiest place to start is the key of A minor, since it produces a minor scale using only the white notes on the keyboard –

This is the *descending* form of the **melodic minor scale**. The *ascending* form sharpens the 6th and 7th degrees –

The other type of minor scale is the **harmonic minor scale**. The notes are the same ascending and descending –

The reason for these differences lies in the fact that *melodies* in a minor key tend to use the sharpened 6th and 7th degrees when they are going up but the unsharpened notes when they are coming down; on the other hand *chords* in a minor key normally use just the unsharpened 6th degree and the sharpened 7th degree. The intervals formed by the first five degrees of the scale (T S T T) never change.

The key signatures of minor keys always comprise the sharps or flats of the descending melodic minor scale. There are none in A minor, so it has no key signature – like C major. Sharps are added to the notes F and G, if needed, as they occur during the course of the music.

Taking another example, here are the various versions of the minor scale starting on E –

E minor (melodic)

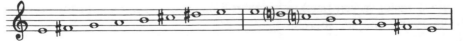

E minor (harmonic)

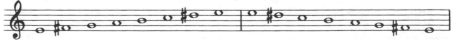

The descending melodic form has an F#, so the key signature for E minor is
F# – the same as for G major. Again, if they are needed, sharps are added to
the 6th and 7th degrees (C and D) as they occur.

As a final example, these are the versions of the minor scale starting on D –

D minor (melodic)

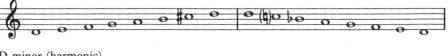

D minor (harmonic)

The descending melodic form has a B♭, so the key signature for D minor is B♭
– the same as for F major. If they are needed, accidentals are added to the 6th
and 7th degrees (B♭/B♮, C♮/C#) as they occur.

A piece of music in a minor key may use the notes of both the melodic and
the harmonic minor scales. Therefore one cannot talk about a piece as being
'in C melodic minor' or 'in C harmonic minor', only as 'in C minor'.

4/3 Relative major/minor keys

Examples of corresponding key signatures for major and minor keys have
already been noted. There is a fixed relationship: the key-note of a minor key is
always the same as the 6th degree of the major scale with the same key
signature, as is shown in the following examples (note that the scales are now
given with their key signatures) –

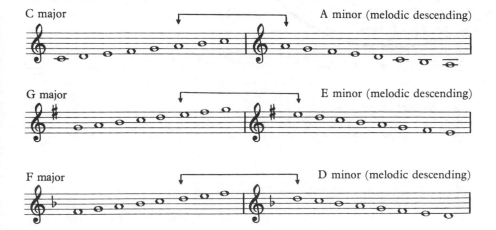

Consequently there is a pattern of minor-key signatures corresponding to the pattern of major-key signatures –

No sharps or flats   A minor   (C major)

1 sharp	(F)	E minor	(G major)
2 sharps	(F C)	B minor	(D major)
3 sharps	(F C G)	F♯ minor	(A major)
4 sharps	(F C G D)	C♯ minor	(E major)
5 sharps	(F C G D A)	G♯ minor	(B major)
6 sharps	(F C G D A E)	D♯ minor	(F♯ major)
1 flat	(B)	D minor	(F major)
2 flats	(B E)	G minor	(B♭ major)
3 flats	(B E A)	C minor	(E♭ major)
4 flats	(B E A D)	F minor	(A♭ major)
5 flats	(B E A D G)	B♭ minor	(D♭ major)
6 flats	(B E A D G C)	E♭ minor	(G♭ major)

On the next page is a complete list of key signatures up to seven sharps or flats. It shows which lines of the stave the sharps and flats are placed on.

Major and minor keys which share the same key signature (e.g. G major and E minor) are said to be 'relatives' of each other: G major, for example, is the **relative major** of E minor, and E minor is the **relative minor** of G major. These expressions have some use as a kind of shorthand, but they can be dangerously misleading, since they may suggest that keys with the same key signature are merely versions of each other. They are not. They have different key-notes. Since (as will be seen shortly) the importance of every other note in a scale depends on its relationship to the key-note, the whole balance of the two keys is quite different. Only keys with the *same* key-note are truly versions of each other (e.g. G major and G minor). To underline this point, here are all the versions of the scale of C (note that not only the key-note but the 2nd, 4th and 5th degrees remain the same throughout) –

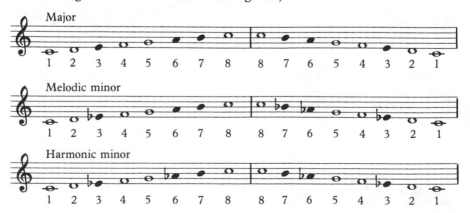

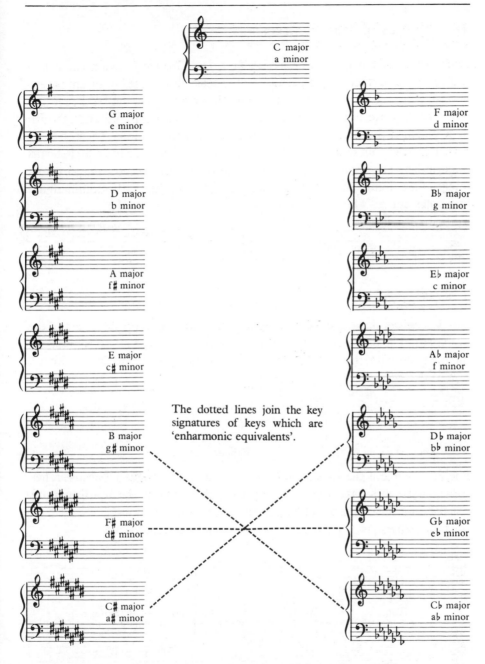

The dotted lines join the key signatures of keys which are 'enharmonic equivalents'.

Note that small letters may be used to distinguish a minor key from a major one, a practice sometimes used in reference books, lists of works etc. However, although writing just 'G' (for major) or 'g' (for minor) certainly saves time and space, it can be ambiguous and should generally be avoided. It is worth adding that in ordinary speech and often in publications, if 'major' or 'minor' is not mentioned, it is to be assumed that the key is major, e.g. Beethoven's Symphony No.7 in A is in A major.

4/4 Names of scale degrees

Each degree of a major or minor scale (1st, 2nd, 3rd etc.) has a name which reflects its importance or its position in the scale. The most important note is naturally the one on which the scale is based: the first note, the 1st degree, the key-note or **tonic**, as it is generally known.[1] But almost as important is the 5th degree, called the **dominant**, which can be said to dominate because of its special relationship with the tonic[2], especially (as will be seen in 9/2b) in terms of harmony. The 4th degree is called the **subdominant** because it is a mirror-image of the dominant, lying five notes *below* the tonic just as the dominant lies five notes above. Thus in C major –

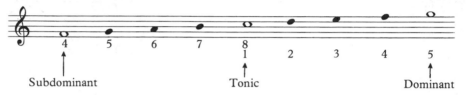

The 3rd degree is the **mediant,** since it lies midway between the tonic and the dominant. The 6th degree is the **submediant** because it is a mirror-image of the mediant, lying the same distance below the tonic as the mediant is above –

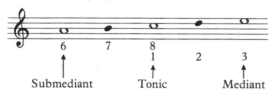

The 2nd degree is the **supertonic** (*super* is Latin for 'above'), because it lies immediately above the tonic. Finally the 7th degree is the **leading note** because in a melody it tends to lead up to the tonic.

These names are applied to both the major and minor scales –

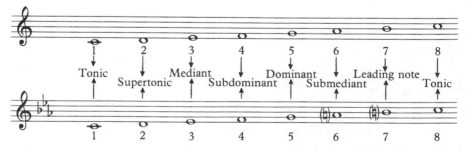

[1]The word ultimately derives from a Greek word meaning 'pitch'; musically it can be thought of as the basic pitch of a piece.
[2]Brass players will know that it is the 'third harmonic', the first two being the 'fundamental' note produced by a length of tubing and the octave above that (see 20/4a in Part II).

In a minor key, 'leading note' by itself implies the *raised* 7th degree (a semitone below the tonic); the lower 7th (as in the key signature) is referred to as the 'flattened leading note'.

4/5 Double sharps and double flats

Before considering other kinds of scale, something must be said about a problem which was lurking in the discussion of minor scales. Sometimes it is necessary to add a further sharp to a note which has already been sharpened, or a further flat to a note which has already been flattened. The scale of G♯ minor, for example, already has an F♯ in the key signature: how then is one to write the 7th degree when it has to be sharpened, as in the melodic minor scale ascending?

What is needed is a sign called a **double sharp** – ⅹ – though it is often written as a small letter 'x', which it closely resembles. Its effect is to raise a note *two* semitones (Cⅹ, for example, sounding the same as the white note D on the keyboard). Thus the notation of the ascending melodic minor scale of G♯ is –

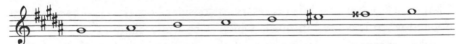

Similarly, there is a **double flat** which lowers a note two semitones, but the sign for this is merely two flats together – ♭♭ . So now we can complete the music example in the middle of p.23.

To cancel a double sharp or a double flat (i.e. to restore the note to its original pitch), all that is needed is a *single* sharp or flat –

Formerly a natural was inserted as well (♮♯ or ♮♭) but this is no longer standard practice (compare changes of key signature in 2/3).

4/6 The chromatic scale

The scales of all major and minor keys are **diatonic** scales. (In a minor key, both the harmonic and melodic forms of the scale are diatonic.) Notes which do not belong to the key (e.g. the C♯s in the first example on p.14) are said to be **chromatic**. A 'chromatic scale' is a scale made up entirely of semitones: one which includes *all* the notes (black and white) on the keyboard. Here is a one-octave chromatic scale starting on D (although, as we shall see shortly, there are other ways of notating it) –

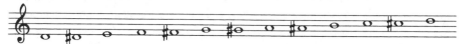

For about three centuries after 1600 music was generally based on the major and minor scales and not on the chromatic scale. Individual chromatic notes were used, but often merely as special effects (the word 'chromatic' means 'coloured') which had no influence upon the key. Sometimes, it is true, their use could bring about a change of key, in which case the key signature might be changed (see Part II, Chapter 16). During the second half of the 19th century and the early part of the 20th, the use of chromatic notes developed to such an extent that any feeling of **tonality** (being in a key) was often weakened. In the hands of some composers, it was finally destroyed altogether (in music described as 'atonal'), although many others have continued to write tonal music. More will be said about atonal music and its notation in Part II, Chapter 24/3, but first it is necessary to consider how the chromatic scale is notated when it is used in music which is basically diatonic.

When chromatic scales, or parts of them, occur in real music (as distinct from theory books!), composers are often not fussy about their notation. Usually they are written in whatever way seems convenient, bearing in mind the key signature if there is one. In practice this generally means using the minimum number of accidentals needed to do the job, though there can be more than one way of achieving this. Here are two examples from piano music by Mozart: the first from the Fantasia in D minor K.397, and the second from the Rondo in D major, K.485 –

In both of these passages the basic chromatic scale (starting on the key note, D, in each case) has been marked. Notice that the first example starts D-Eb-E♮, but that the second starts D-D♯-E (which is also the way the first example ends). Both use A-Bb-B♮ (not A-A♯-B as opposite).

Theorists distinguish between two ways of writing the chromatic scale: the harmonic and the melodic (or 'arbitrary'). These are described below, but no one need lose any sleep over them since composers themselves never have.

The **harmonic chromatic scale** is the same whether ascending or descending, and whether it occurs in a major or in a minor key. It includes all the notes of the major *and* minor scales (both harmonic and melodic), plus the flattened 2nd and sharpened 4th degrees. In practice this always means that every degree of the scale has to be written twice, except the 5th and, of course, the key-note at the top and bottom, e.g. –

D major

D minor

Melodic chromatic scales are less rigid in their construction: in fact, theorists do not invariably agree exactly *how* they are formed. What may be said is that they differ in their ascending and descending versions, and also according to whether the key is major or minor. Perhaps the simplest way of forming them is to include, first, all the notes of the key (in a minor key these include the notes of both the melodic and harmonic scales). The additional notes are then provided by sharpening the diatonic notes (where required) in the ascending form, or by flattening them in the descending form, e.g. –

D major

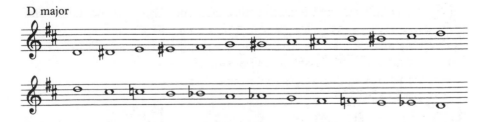

D minor

Some authorities, however, would always use the 7th degree twice – e.g. C♮ (not B♯) in the ascending scale in D major; and some would include the sharpened 4th rather than the flattened 5th (G♯ rather than A♭) in both descending scales. One principle which all would accept is that the same letter name must never be used more than twice in succession: thus A♭ – A♮ – A♯, for example, would always be wrong.

4/7 C clefs

The extensive use of ledger lines is a relatively recent development: the further back one goes in musical history the rarer they become. Earlier composers avoided them by changing the clef. For example, both the G and F clefs, and , were also positioned on other lines, and , which then denoted G and F respectively.

Even more mobile was a clef we have not yet encountered – the **C clef**. This was always centred on a line and indicated middle C. Originally it could be placed on any of the first four lines of the stave, but nowadays it is used only on the third and fourth – . The note in brackets is middle C. Thus these passages all sound exactly the same –

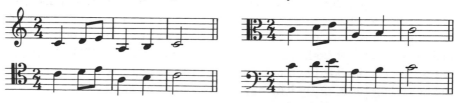

is generally referred to as the 'alto' clef, and as the 'tenor' clef.

Today they are scarcely ever used for vocal music, but, as will be seen in Part II, some orchestral instruments use them.

Key signatures in these clefs are arranged thus –

CHAPTER 5

The Grouping of Notes and Rests

5/1 Note groupings in simple (♩) and compound (♩.) time

SIMPLE TIME   The standard practice is to avoid ties where possible. (Bear in mind that ties join *notes of the same pitch* – see 3/2.) Thus ♫. is better than ♫♩ ; ♫♫ or ♫♩ would be worse! Likewise –

Quavers should be beamed together: up to a complete bar in ²₄ |♫♫| or ³₄ |♫♫♫|, and up to half a bar in ⁴₄ |♫♫♩| or |♩ ♫♫|. They are not normally beamed across the middle of the bar in ⁴₄, so ⁴₄ ♩ ♫♫♩ | is NOT standard practice: ⁴₄ ♩ ♫ ♫♩ | is to be preferred. In ³₄ a dotted crotchet followed by three quavers is best grouped ³₄ ♩. ♪♫| (it is true that they are frequently written ³₄ ♩. ♫♫| instead, but that grouping may cause confusion since it suggests ⁶₈ not ³₄).

Notes shorter than quavers are beamed together in beats –

²₄ 𝅘𝅥𝅯𝅘𝅥𝅯𝅘𝅥𝅯 𝅘𝅥𝅯𝅘𝅥𝅯𝅘𝅥𝅯| ²₄ ♩. 𝅘𝅥𝅯𝅘𝅥𝅯 |𝅘𝅥𝅯𝅘𝅥𝅯♩ |

However, demisemiquavers may also be grouped in half-beats –

²₄ 𝅘𝅥𝅰𝅘𝅥𝅰𝅘𝅥𝅰𝅘𝅥𝅰 𝅘𝅥𝅰𝅘𝅥𝅰𝅘𝅥𝅰𝅘𝅥𝅰| ²₄ 𝅘𝅥𝅰𝅘𝅥𝅰𝅘𝅥𝅰 𝅘𝅥𝅰𝅘𝅥𝅰𝅘𝅥𝅰 𝅘𝅥𝅰𝅘𝅥𝅰𝅘𝅥𝅰 𝅘𝅥𝅰𝅘𝅥𝅰𝅘𝅥𝅰|

There are other ways of writing the same thing –

²₄ 𝅘𝅥𝅰𝅘𝅥𝅰𝅘𝅥𝅰𝅘𝅥𝅰𝅘𝅥𝅰𝅘𝅥𝅰𝅘𝅥𝅰𝅘𝅥𝅰| 𝅘𝅥𝅰𝅘𝅥𝅰𝅘𝅥𝅰𝅘𝅥𝅰𝅘𝅥𝅰𝅘𝅥𝅰𝅘𝅥𝅰𝅘𝅥𝅰|

COMPOUND TIME   Notes lasting two beats are usually written 𝅗𝅥. rather than
𝅗𝅥. 𝅗𝅥. in compound time –

[musical examples: 6/8 and 9/8 time signatures showing correct vs NOT groupings]

Notes lasting a full bar in 9/8 and 12/8 are written –

[musical examples: 9/8 and 12/8 time signatures]

Apart from the above, however, compound time rhythms are written so
that the eye can easily pick out where the beats occur. This means that tied
notes often *have* to be used –

[musical examples: 6/8, 8 and 9/8 time signatures showing correct vs NOT]

Similarly, quavers and shorter notes are beamed so as to show the division
of beats –

[musical examples: 6/8 time signatures showing beaming]

5/2 Rest groupings in simple (𝄽) and compound (𝄾·) time

SIMPLE TIME   The general rule is that every beat should have a rest of its own –

[musical examples: 2/4, 2/4, 3/4, 3/4 time signatures]

So long as this rule is complied with, as few rests as possible should be used –

[musical examples: 2/4, 2/4 time signatures]

In quadruple time, however, a 2-beat rest should be used for either half of the bar but not in the middle. Thus $\frac{4}{4}$ ▬ 𝅗𝅥 | and $\frac{4}{4}$ 𝅗𝅥 ▬ | are correct; but $\frac{4}{4}$ 𝅗𝅥 ▬ 𝅗𝅥 | is wrong: it should be $\frac{4}{4}$ 𝅗𝅥 𝄽 𝄽 𝅗𝅥 |. Similarly, $\frac{4}{4}$ 𝅗𝅥 𝄽 ▬ | cannot be replaced by $\frac{4}{4}$ 𝅗𝅥 ▬· |. Less unsatisfactory is $\frac{4}{4}$ ▬· 𝅗𝅥 | but the conventional notation is $\frac{4}{4}$ ▬ 𝄽 𝅗𝅥 |.

Halving the notes and rests in the $\frac{2}{4}$ patterns at the bottom of p.34 (♪ 𝄾 𝄽 and 𝄽 𝄾 ♪) shows how semiquaver rests are arranged when they occur as part of a 𝅗𝅥 beat: ♪ 𝄿 𝄾 and 𝄾 𝄿 ♪ . (Similarly, a further subdivision will show how demisemiquaver rests are grouped.) In other words, the rests correspond with the subdivisions of the beat: $\frac{2}{4}$ ♪𝄿 𝄾 𝄾 𝄿 ♪ . However, not all modern composers invariably follow the orthodox procedures in this respect: 𝄾· ♪ is sometimes to be found instead of the 'correct' 𝄾 𝄿 ♪ , and ♪𝄾· instead of ♪𝄿 𝄾 . It cannot be denied that $\frac{2}{4}$ ♪𝄾· 𝄾· ♪ is both unambiguous and easier to read than $\frac{2}{4}$ ♪𝄿 𝄾 𝄾 𝄿 ♪ .

COMPOUND TIME   In $\frac{6}{8}$, $\frac{9}{8}$ or $\frac{12}{8}$, a silence which lasts one complete beat can be shown as *either* 𝄽· *or* 𝄽 𝄾 . If only the first two quavers of a dotted crotchet beat are silent, they are best shown as 𝄽 ♪ , though they are sometimes written as 𝄾 𝄾 ♪ ; but if the *last* two quavers of a dotted crotchet beat are silent, they should always be shown as ♪𝄾 𝄾 (♪𝄽 is incorrect). Thus one may think of the three units of a compound-time beat as being grouped 2 + 1, like a crotchet and a dot, not as 1 + 2. The way the rests are grouped in this example demonstrates the standard practice –

$\frac{6}{8}$ 𝄽 ♪♪𝄾 𝄾 | ♪𝄾 𝄾 𝄽 ♪| ♪♪♪𝄽 |

Otherwise, everything that was said about rests in simple time can be applied to rests in compound time, bearing in mind the general rule that 'every beat should have a rest of its own' now refers to a dotted note (𝅘𝅥.) –

$\frac{6}{8}$ 𝅘𝅥 𝄾 𝄽 | OR 𝅘𝅥 𝄾 𝄽 𝄾 | NOT 𝅘𝅥 𝄽 𝄽 | NOR 𝅘𝅥 ▬ |

$\frac{6}{8}$ ♪𝄾 𝄾 𝄽 | OR ♪𝄾 𝄾 𝄽 𝄾 | NOT ♪𝄽 𝄽 | NOR ♪𝄾 ▬ |

$\frac{9}{8}$ 𝄽 𝄽 𝅘𝅥. | OR 𝄽 𝄾 𝄽 𝄾 𝅘𝅥. | NOT ▬· 𝅘𝅥. |

$\frac{9}{8}$ 𝅘𝅥. 𝄽 𝄽 | OR 𝅘𝅥. 𝄽 𝄾 𝄽 𝄾 | NOT 𝅘𝅥. ▬· |

$\frac{12}{8}$ 𝅘𝅥. 𝄽 𝄽 𝅘𝅥. | OR 𝅘𝅥. 𝄽 𝄾 𝄽 𝄾 𝅘𝅥. | NOT 𝅘𝅥. ▬· 𝅘𝅥. |

Similarly, when either half of a $\frac{12}{8}$ bar is silent, a $-$ rest should be used –

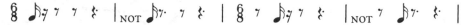

Rests forming part of a compound-time beat ($\downarrow$.) invariably follow the simple-time conventions explained previously, i.e. the subdivisions of the beat must be shown. Hence –

The following quotations illustrate points made so far –

(Allegro)   Beethoven, Violin Sonata in D (Rondo)

Allegro vivace   Mozart, 'Jupiter' Symphony (1st mvt)

J. S. Bach, Toccata & Fugue in C for organ

and

(Moderato)   Elgar, Cello Concerto (1st mvt)

Beams may be continued over rests occurring in a group of quavers or shorter notes. Most commonly they are used over a single rest, as in the examples on p.19 and in the quotation from Sibelius on p.37.

5/3 Groupings in other time signatures

Everything that was said earlier about the grouping of notes and rests assumed that the beat was a $\downarrow$ in simple time ($\frac{2}{4}$, $\frac{3}{4}$, $\frac{4}{4}$) and a $\downarrow$. in compound time ($\frac{6}{8}$, $\frac{9}{8}$, $\frac{12}{8}$). But as has already been explained, a beat can be represented in other ways, e.g. as a $\downarrow$ in simple time ($\frac{2}{2}$, $\frac{3}{2}$, $\frac{4}{2}$) or a $\flat$ ($\frac{2}{8}$, $\frac{3}{8}$, $\frac{4}{8}$). Similarly, in compound time the beat could be a $\downarrow$. ($\frac{6}{4}$, $\frac{9}{4}$, $\frac{12}{4}$) or a $\flat$ ($\frac{6}{16}$, $\frac{9}{16}$, $\frac{12}{16}$). The conventions about grouping are unchanged when these equivalent time signatures are used. Consequently, the examples which have already been given still apply, but the values of the notes and rests must be doubled or halved to conform with the equivalent time signatures. For example –

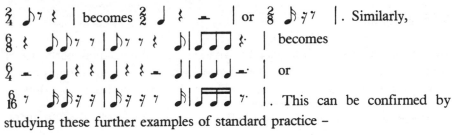

becomes. Similarly, becomes or. This can be confirmed by studying these further examples of standard practice –

Gigue — J. S. Bach, Partita in D for keyboard

(Allegro) — Sibelius, Symphony No.1 (1st mvt)

Copyright Breitkopf & Härtel, Wiesbaden

(Lento) — Delius, Violin Sonata No.2

The grouping of notes and rests in bars of five or seven beats (quintuple or septuple time) is a problem of a different kind. Bars such as these, in practice, are almost always understood by the listener as combinations of two and three beats: 5 as 2 + 3 or 3 + 2; and 7 as 2 + 2 (or 4) + 3, or 2 + 3 + 2 etc. The following familiar themes from the 2nd movement of Tchaikovsky's 6th Symphony are typical examples (both are made up of bars of 2 + 3 beats) –

(Allegro con grazia)

In such cases, the grouping of the notes and rests corresponds with the subdivisions of the bar, as in the oboe melody at the opening of the 4th movement (*Intermezzo Interrotto*) in Bartók's *Concerto for Orchestra* –

Allegretto

5/4 Duplets

Just as a simple-time beat can be divided into three equal parts, so in compound time a beat can be divided into a group of two equal notes called a **duplet**. They are sometimes shown by the addition of dots – ♪♪♪ ♪♪. | (♪. ♪. = ♪♪♪) , but it is more usual to show them by the figure *2* – ♪♪♪ ♪♪ | as in this example –

(Allegro non troppo)   Tchaikovsky, *Serenade for Strings* (1st mvt)

etc.

Triplets and duplets can both be thought of as irregular rhythmic groups since they go against the normal pattern: a triplet is a division into three where a division into two would be normal; a duplet is a division into two where three would be normal.

5/5 Other irregular time divisions

Basically, any time value can normally be divided either into two or into three equal parts. This is not merely a matter of a simple or compound time signature. As already mentioned, divisions into three are not restricted to compound time but can also occur in simple time (i.e. triplets), e.g. ♩ ♪♪♪ | ♩ ♪♪♪♪ | ♩ ♩ ♩ | . Similarly, divisions into two can be found in compound time ♩. ♪♪ | ; and so can further triplet subdivisions ♩. ♪♪♪♪ | .

An irregular rhythmic group, therefore, is one which does not correspond with the 'normal' division into two or three.

5/5a Irregular divisions of simple time values

The following examples illustrate how a note value which normally subdivides into 2 (e.g. ♩) may be subdivided into irregular groups of 3, 5, 6 etc. –

In each of these examples, the irregular group takes the time of one crotchet. Note, however, the time values employed: 3 (triplet) are written as quavers; 5 (quintuplet), 6 (sextuplet) and 7 (septuplet) are written as semiquavers, while 9 (no special name is used) are written as demi-semiquavers. To sum up: when a time value which would normally divide into 2 is divided into an irregular group of equal notes –

3 notes are written in the values appropriate to 2 of the same kind;
5, 6, 7 notes are written in the values appropriate to 4 of the same kind;
9, 10, 11, 13, 15 notes are written in the values appropriate to 8 of the same kind;
17, 19 etc. notes are written in the values appropriate to 16 of the same kind;

Thus, a group of 5 notes in the time of a crotchet uses the values it would if there were only 4 of them, i.e. semiquavers. Similarly, a group of 9 uses the values it would if there were only 8 of them, i.e. demisemiquavers. If they were performed in the time of a *minim*, however, a group of 5 would be written as quavers and a group of 9 as semiquavers, e.g. –

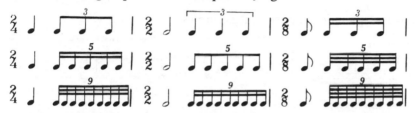

The quotations below are typical examples of how composers have used and notated irregular rhythmic groups –

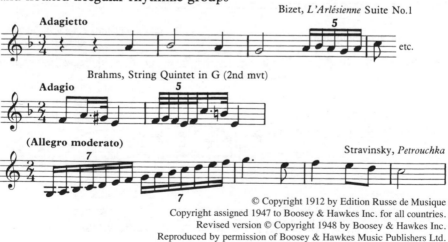

Bizet, *L'Arlésienne* Suite No.1

Adagietto

etc.

Brahms, String Quintet in G (2nd mvt)

Adagio

(Allegro moderato)

Stravinsky, *Petrouchka*

(Moderato con anima)   Tchaikovsky, Symphony No.5 (2nd mvt)

5/5b Irregular divisions of compound time values

As we have seen, when a ♩. beat is subdivided into two equal parts, they may be written ♩♩. or ♪♪ . However, composers have sometimes used yet another method, and have been even less consistent about the notation of other irregular compound time values. The most common occurrences can be summarised as follows –

The following quotations are typical examples –

(Assez vif)   Debussy, String Quartet (2nd mvt)

(Allegro con fuoco)   Brahms, Piano Sonata No.1 (Finale)

(Allegro tranquillo)   Vaughan Williams, *The Lark Ascending*

© 1925 by Oxford University Press
Reproduced by permission.

(Lento)   Schumann, Fantasy in C

(Allegro)   Holst, *The Planets* ('Uranus')

The situation becomes even more involved when smaller subdivisions are used, but since they are relatively rare they need not be explained at this stage: full details are given in Appendix A.

CHAPTER 6

Rhythm: Words, Syncopation

6/1 Rhythmic notation of words

When music is set to words, they are placed immediately under the notes to which they belong. A recent practice, now accepted as standard, is for notes to be beamed together rhythmically according to the conventions described in Chapter 5, e.g. –

Handel, *Messiah*

For un-to us a child is born, un-to us a son is given

although formerly they would have been written with every syllable under a separately stemmed note –

For un-to us a child is born, un-to us a son is given

The ⌢ sign over 'born' (not to be confused with a 'tie', which has a different function – see 3/2) indicates that the two notes are to be sung to the same syllable. It is not strictly necessary in the second example, since beaming the notes together serves the same purpose. The older method is still commonly found – as, for example, in most of the vocal passages quoted in this book, which follow the original notation. However, there is no doubt that the new one makes the music easier to read. Compare, for example, Sullivan's notation of this phrase from *The Mikado* –

The sun whose rays are all a-blaze with ev-er liv-ing glo – ry

with the way it would be written today –

The sun whose rays are all a-blaze with ev-er liv-ing glo – ry

In some foreign languages, particularly Italian, a vowel at the end of a word is sometimes combined with one at the beginning of the next word. The two vowels are usually joined with a tie, e.g. 'rimanti in' becomes 'rimanti in'. This process is called an 'elision': the two vowels are said to be 'elided'. The combined vowels become a single sound and are given one note, as in bar 3 of this example –

Monteverdi, *L'incoronazione di Poppea*

Pop – pe – a,   ri – man – ti in pa – – ce;

6/2 Setting word rhythms to music

In speaking, two things can affect the meaning of a word or a group of words. The first is whether the voice rises or falls, or stays level. In asking a question, for example, the pitch normally goes up at the end: compare how one says the word 'tomorrow' in these two sentences – 'Are you coming tomorrow?' and 'You must come tomorrow'. Even more important to meaning is the way in which syllables are accented. 'Refuse', for example, can mean two quite different things, depending on which of the two syllables is stressed: 'réfuse' (the accent marks the stress) is a noun meaning 'rubbish' or 'litter'; 'refúse' is a verb meaning 'reject', 'not accept' etc.

Indeed, accenting different words in a sentence can give it different shades of meaning, even though the words themselves are unchanged. The phrase, 'I will go', can have varied implications according to which of the words is emphasised. These are suggested below by the words in brackets, although in spoken language emphasis alone is sufficient –

I (myself) will go.
I wíll go (and nothing will stop me).
I will gó (but I may not come back).

When words are set to music, the accented syllables are normally put on accented beats and weak syllables on weak beats. So 'I will go' needs different rhythms according to which sense is intended –

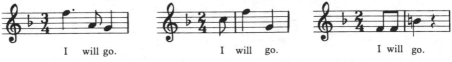

I   will go.   I   will   go.   I will   go.

Accents in words are called 'verbal accents'. On the opposite page are some examples to demonstrate the usual ways in which verbal and musical accents coincide.

(a) Leonard Bernstein, *West Side Story*

Moderato con anima

Ma – ri – a!___ I've just met a girl named Ma –

-ri–a,___ And suddenly that name Will ne-ver be the same to me.

(b) Christmas hymn

O come, all ye faith – ful, Joy-ful and tri – um – phant, O

come ye, O come_ ye to Beth – le –hem.

(c) (Allegro grazioso) Sullivan, *The Yeomen of the Guard*

Were I thy bride, then all the world be - side were not too

wide To hold my wealth of love. Were I thy bride!

(d) Purcell, *Dido and Aeneas*

Thy hand, Bel-in – da! dark – – – ness shades me, On thy

bo – som let me rest; More I would, but Death in-

-vades me; Death_ is now_ a wel – come_ guest.

Making musical accents coincide with the verbal accents is the primary way of showing the latter, but it is not the only way. In the three settings of 'I will go', the *shape* of the melodies helped to achieve the emphasis which was needed – e.g. the move upwards to a high note on 'will' in the second of the three. Another way is to use a long note or a group of notes for an accented syllable (as on 'darkness' in the Purcell example above). A long note amidst short ones is always likely to seem accented (a type of accent called an 'agogic' accent), as in this setting by Britten of words by Tennyson –

Here the relatively long notes on 'splen-', 'falls', 'long', 'shakes' and 'glo-' give them an accent although none of them coincides with a 'strong' beat; similarly, the group of notes on 'leaps'. (A group of notes on one syllable is called a **melisma**.) Again, the shape of the melody helps: e.g. the leap upwards to the first syllable of 'splendour'; the more gradual ascents to 'old', 'shakes' and 'cataract'; and the falls to the weak final syllables of 'story' and 'glory'.

6/3 Syncopation

Accenting a note which would normally be unaccented is called **syncopation**. Syncopated rhythms are felt to go against a regular pattern of strong and weak beats (as indicated by the time signature). They are easy to spot when they occur in vocal music, as in this opening of a Negro spiritual –

'Name' is a word which demands to be accented, yet every time it occurs off the beat, at a point in the bar which would otherwise not have been stressed.

Here is another example of syncopation in vocal music –

Walton, *Belshazzar's Feast*

Then sing_____ a-loud to God _ our strength:

The accents are shown by > signs; *sf* and *sfz* can also be used for this purpose (see 10/2). They reinforce the syncopated effect produced by the coincidence of strong syllables with weak beats ('-loud', 'God'); and they also create syncopations in the long melisma on 'sing' by stressing weak parts of bar 3.

The following passage from Beethoven's Piano Sonata Op.2 No.3 (first movement), is an example of syncopation in instrumental music. The music in the bass clef is completely regular, in conformity with the time signature, but the notes in the treble clef include accents on beats (2 and 4) which are normally weak.

[Allegro con brio]

In this last example, the regular pattern of strong and weak beats was maintained (in the left hand) during the syncopation in the right hand. Sometimes, however, the regular pattern is suspended completely, as in the next extract, from another Beethoven Piano Sonata: Op.27 No.1 (last movement). Now, neither hand maintains the regular pattern –

[Allegro vivace]

Notice not only that the syncopations are shown by *sf* signs, but also that the composer underlines the point by beaming notes across bar-lines. Although the regular pattern of accents is suspended completely in the example above, it had previously been firmly fixed in the listener's mind. Thus the passage beginning with the first *sf* is felt as a disturbance: in other words, it is felt to be syncopated. In music where there is no regular pattern of strong and weak beats (as in the Bartók melody quoted on p.37) there can be no syncopation.

CHAPTER 7

Intervals and Transposition

7/1 Intervals within an octave

An **interval** is the distance in pitch between any two notes. If the two notes are played together –  – they form a 'harmonic interval'; if one comes after the other – or – it is a 'melodic interval'. We have already seen one example: the octave (see 2/1), i.e. the distance from any note to the next note with the same name.

In counting the notes of intervals, both notes are included. C to D, for example, is a 2nd; C to E a 3rd; C to F a 4th, and so on. Intervals are described more fully than this, however: not only by their 'number' but also by their 'quality'. The interval from a key-note to the 5th note above it (the dominant), for instance, is not just a '5th' but a 'perfect 5th'. The following example shows the full names of all the intervals between the key-note of a major key (in this case, C major) and each of the other degrees –

| major 2nd | major 3rd | perfect 4th | perfect 5th | major 6th | major 7th | perfect 8ve |

The same intervals are of course produced by any other major key: e.g. in A♭ major –

| major 2nd | major 3rd | perfect 4th | perfect 5th | major 6th | major 7th | perfect 8ve |

In a minor key, some intervals from the key-note are identical with those from the key-note of the major key with the same tonic, namely the 2nd, 4th, 5th and 8ve. Since they are identical, they keep the same names: e.g. in C minor –

| major 2nd | perfect 4th | perfect 5th | perfect 8ve |

The 3rd, however, is different and therefore needs a new name. It is called a 'minor 3rd' –

The intervals of the 6th and 7th may or may not be different, depending on which form of the minor scale (melodic or harmonic) is used. If (as in the *ascending* melodic minor scale) they are the same as in the major scale, they keep the same names –

major major
6th 7th

But the descending form of the melodic minor scale produces two new intervals, the 'minor 6th' and 'minor 7th' –

The following example now assembles all the intervals produced by the major and minor scales based on one key-note: in this case, C –

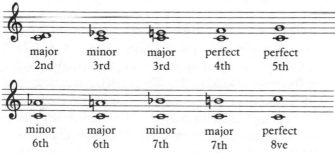

| major | minor | major | perfect | perfect |
| 2nd | 3rd | 3rd | 4th | 5th |

| minor | major | minor | major | perfect |
| 6th | 6th | 7th | 7th | 8ve |

The intervals illustrated above are those produced by the major and minor scales; as such they are called 'diatonic intervals'. All others are 'chromatic intervals'. In the series of intervals based on C, for example, two possibilities were not included –

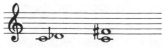

because neither D♭ nor F♯ appears in the major or minor scales on C. They are therefore chromatic intervals. But that does not tell us what their individual names are, nor do we yet have names for the intervals formed by enharmonic changes. What, for example, do we call this minor 7th –

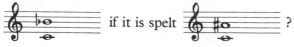

if it is spelt ?

The answers to these problems can be summarised –

If the upper note of a perfect or major interval is raised a semitone, the interval becomes **augmented**;

if the upper note of a minor interval is raised a semitone, it becomes major;

if the upper note of a perfect or minor interval is lowered a semitone, it becomes **diminished**;

if the upper note of a major interval is lowered a semitone, it becomes minor.

Thus, if the upper note of a perfect 4th – e.g. 𝄞 – is raised a semitone – 𝄞 – it becomes an augmented 4th. Similarly, if the upper note of a major 2nd – e.g. 𝄞 – is lowered a semitone – 𝄞 – it becomes a minor 2nd. But when 𝄞 is re-spelt as 𝄞 it changes not only its quality but its number. C to B-anything is always a 7th of some kind, but C to A-anything must be some kind of 6th. Since the A♯ is the raised form of the 6th degree of the major scale on C, the C to A♯ above is an augmented 6th.

The interval of the minor 2nd, e.g. C to D♭ as above, raises yet another problem: what would it be called if it were spelt enharmonically – C to C♯? It cannot be any kind of a 2nd, because a 2nd must be C to D-something (♭, ♯, ♮ etc.). C to C♯ must logically be some kind of '1st', though it is never described in this way. The word used instead of '1st' is **unison**: if two instruments play exactly the same note they are said to be 'in unison' (the word literally means 'one sound'). The unison can be thought of as a 'perfect' interval, like the 8ve, i.e. it becomes augmented if one of its notes is raised a semitone –

𝄞 . However it is spelt, this interval remains a semitone, but C to C♯ is a 'chromatic semitone' while C to D♭ is a 'diatonic semitone'. (C and C♯ do not co-exist in any major or minor scale, but C and D♭ are found together in several: e.g. A♭ major.)

Intervals of a 2nd, 3rd, 6th and 7th can therefore be: DIMINISHED, MINOR, MAJOR or AUGMENTED; but the intervals of a 4th, 5th, 8ve and also the unison, can only be: DIMINISHED, PERFECT or AUGMENTED. This is all summed up in the table of intervals, based on C, on the next page. The arrows connect intervals which sound the same but are spelt differently, i.e. intervals which are enharmonic equivalents.

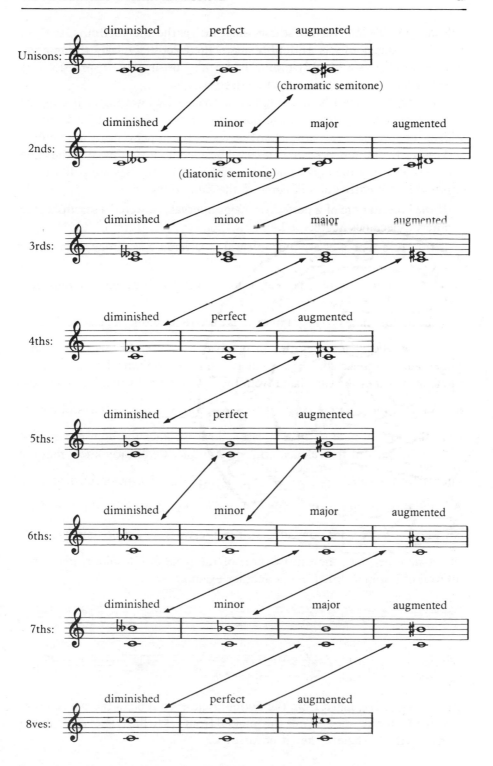

Some possible intervals are still missing, such as the interval from C to D × . Strictly speaking, this is a 'doubly-augmented 2nd'; similarly the interval from C to G♭♭ is a 'doubly-diminished 5th'. Fortunately, in practice it is rarely necessary to venture into such deep waters.

An interval can also be made larger or smaller by lowering or raising the *bottom* note. Clearly, lowering the bottom note of an interval by a semitone widens it to precisely the same extent as raising the upper note by a semitone; and raising the bottom note of an interval by a semitone narrows it to the same extent as lowering the upper note by a semitone. So the 'Ifs' on p.48 can be expressed differently but still come to the same thing –

If the bottom note of a perfect or major interval is lowered a semitone, the interval becomes augmented;

if the bottom note of a minor interval is lowered a semitone, it becomes major;

if the bottom note of a perfect or minor interval is raised a semitone, it becomes diminished;

if the bottom note of a major interval is raised a semitone, it becomes minor.

When we begin to apply this in practice, however, the matter becomes rather more complicated. It is absolutely fundamental to the description of all intervals that they are calculated from the *bottom* note. Even if it is a melodic interval and the top note occurs first – e.g. ⟨music⟩ – one still counts from the bottom note (F in this case). So if we alter the bottom note, we change the basis of the calculation. For example, we already know that the interval from F to A – ⟨music⟩ or ⟨music⟩ – is a major third, because A is the third degree of the scale of F major. But if we raise the F to F♯ – ⟨music⟩ – we must now calculate the interval from a scale starting on F♯: the A now becomes the third degree of the scale of F♯ minor, hence the interval of a minor 3rd. Here is another example –

An interval is calculated from the bottom note even though the bottom note may not be the key-note. Thus the interval from C♯ to the A above it is always a minor 6th in whatever key it occurs, e.g. –

because it is always described *as though* the bottom note were the key-note. In the above examples the bottom note is always C♯, and the A above it is found in the minor (not the major) scale on C♯ –

As a final illustration, the first two notes of this theme (in D♭ major) from Tchaikovsky's Fantasy Overture *Romeo and Juliet* –

form the interval of a minor 6th: the interval is counted from the lower of the two notes, C; and A♭ is a minor 6th above the C –  (as in the scale of C harmonic minor).

7/2 Transposition

If this scale of C major –

is written with all the notes an octave lower –

it is said to have been 'transposed': here it was transposed 'down an octave'. Similarly, if this scale of B minor (melodic) –

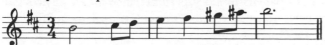

is transposed 'up an octave' it will become –

Moving a series of notes, each the same distance, is called **transposition**. Transposing up or down one or more octaves is the easiest kind of

transposition, because all the notes keep their same names when they are
moved. But music can be transposed to *any* interval. This series of notes –

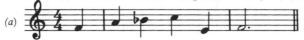

if transposed up a tone (= up a major 2nd) would become –

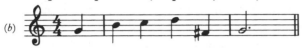

or if transposed down a minor 3rd –

In (*b*) each note is a tone higher than the corresponding note in (*a*); in (*c*) each
note is a minor 3rd lower than in (*a*). The melodic intervals (e.g. the major 3rd
between the first two notes) therefore remain the same. Example (*a*) is in the
key of F major, therefore (*b*) is in G major, and (*c*) in D major. Written with
their appropriate key signatures, the three examples become –

Any accidentals which occur in the original may or may not need to be
changed in a transposed version. Compare what happens if this passage in
G minor –

is transposed into F minor –

The C sharp (sharpened 4th in G minor) becomes B *natural* (sharpened 4th in
F minor). Similarly, the F sharp (leading-note) becomes E natural, although
the flat at the start of the last bar (flattened supertonic) in G minor stays flat in
F minor. Had the piece been transposed into B minor (i.e. up a major 3rd), the
A flat would have become C *natural* –

7/3 Compound intervals

The numbering of intervals continues in exactly the same way after the octave (8th): e.g. in C major –

2nd 3rd 4th 5th 6th 7th 8ve 9th 10th 11th 12th 13th 14th 15th

Thus an interval of an 8ve plus a 5th is a 12th (not a 13th), and an interval of two 8ves is a 15th. Intervals of more than an octave are known as **compound intervals**: a major 10th, for example, can be called a 'compound major 3rd'.

Compound intervals have the same qualities (major, minor etc.) as the corresponding intervals within an octave –

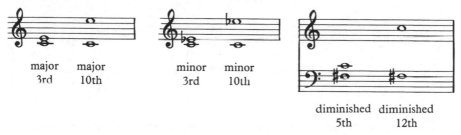

major   major   minor   minor
3rd   10th   3rd   10th

diminished diminished
5th   12th

7/4 Inversion of intervals

Here are two fragments of melody, A and B –

When they are played together they form harmonic intervals –

maj. perf. min. perf. maj.   maj. min. maj. maj. min.
3rd 4th 6th 5th   3rd   6th 7th 3rd 2nd 6th

If B is written an octave higher and then combined with A, the two melodies will still sound well together, but the resulting harmonic intervals are different –

min. perf. maj. perf.   min.   min. maj. min. min. maj.
6th   5th 3rd 4th   6th   3rd 2nd 6th 7th   3rd

(Not all pairs of melodies can be interchanged in this way. When they can, they are said to be 'invertible'.)

The same intervals can of course also be produced by playing A an octave lower and combining it with B –

The intervals of the $\begin{smallmatrix}B\\A\end{smallmatrix}$ combinations are described as **inversions** of the $\begin{smallmatrix}A\\B\end{smallmatrix}$ original. So an interval is inverted when one of its notes is placed above or below the other by being moved up or down an octave. For example,

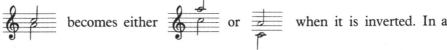 becomes either ... or ... when it is inverted. In a compound interval, however, one note has to be moved *two* octaves for there to be an inversion. If the A in this interval ... is moved down an octave, there is no inversion because the A is still *above* the D. The A must be moved down two octaves to *below* the D – ... – for the interval to be inverted; alternatively, the D may be moved up two octaves to *above* the A –

 .

On the next page is a list of the more common intervals (based on the chromatic scale, with some enharmonic alternatives) and their inversions. It is not as comprehensive as the list of intervals on p.49 but it illustrates all the essential points –

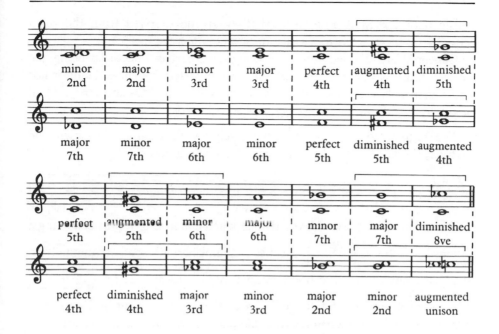

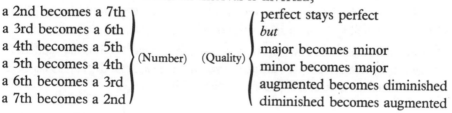

The conclusions to be drawn from this list can be summarised thus –
When an interval is inverted,

a 2nd becomes a 7th ⎫   ⎧ perfect stays perfect
a 3rd becomes a 6th ⎪   ⎪ *but*
a 4th becomes a 5th ⎪   ⎪ major becomes minor
a 5th becomes a 4th ⎬ (Number) (Quality) ⎨ minor becomes major
a 6th becomes a 3rd ⎪   ⎪ augmented becomes diminished
a 7th becomes a 2nd ⎭   ⎩ diminished becomes augmented

7/5 Concords and discords

Both 'concord' and 'discord' are words frequently used outside music, with
very broad meanings; and even in musical contexts, 'discord' in particular is
often employed very loosely. When someone describes a piece of music as
'discordant', that is usually no more than an expression of personal taste; it has
to be remembered that ideas about whether certain sounds are pleasing or not
have varied greatly during the course of musical history. Much music, now
unhesitatingly accepted as sweet and well-mannered, was once thought harsh
and violent.

However, both words are also used in a precise, technical sense. It is true
that these meanings have sometimes changed over the centuries and that they
continue to evolve, but their application to tonal music is agreed. In such

music both **concord** and **discord** (they are not derived from the word 'chord') are terms used to classify harmonic intervals.

Concords are divided into two categories: perfect concords, being the perfect intervals of a 4th, 5th and 8ve; and imperfect concords, being major and minor 3rds and 6ths. All other intervals – i.e. all 2nds and 7ths, and all augmented and diminished intervals – are discords.

The augmented 4th is a particular discord with a name of its own, the **tritone,** so called because it embraces three whole tones –

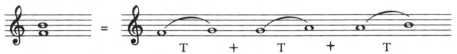

The same interval is still called a tritone when it is inverted, thus becoming a diminished 5th – ♪ because a diminished 5th is an augmented 4th spelt differently (an enharmonic equivalent) – ♪ or ♪ .

The interval between the 4th and 7th degrees of the major and harmonic minor scales is always a tritone, regardless of which note is at the bottom: e.g. in C major and C minor – ♪ ♪ . In the Middle Ages, when the tritone was thought to be very unpleasant, it was referred to as *diabolus in musica* – the devil in music!

What characterises a discord (or a 'dissonant' interval as it is also called) is that one of its notes seems to want to move up or down one degree, so that the interval becomes a concord (either perfect or imperfect) –

Concords, in comparison, do not need this 'resolution': perfect concords are completely stable, imperfect concords reasonably stable. That, at least, is the theory. Unfortunately for theory, one so-called perfect concord – the perfect 4th – often seems to need a resolution: ♪ . This matter will be returned to in Part II, Chapter 16/4, but the essential point is that a 4th between *upper* notes in a chord is relatively stable, e.g. ♪ , whereas a 4th from the *lowest* note is not – e.g. ♪ . The last chord, for example, suggests the continuation: ♪ .

CHAPTER 8

Triads and Chords

8/1 Triads

What distinguishes Western music more than anything else from other musical traditions is that it is made up of mixtures of simultaneous sounds of different pitch (**harmony**), often combined in very complex ways. (This has been achieved at a price: in comparison with other musical cultures, e.g. that of India, Western music is relatively limited in rhythmic and melodic subtlety.) Two notes forming a harmonic interval (as described in Chapter 7) are the simplest example of different notes performed together. The next most simple combination is the triad, which – as its name implies – consists of three notes.

These three are the note on which the triad is based (the **root**) plus the 3rd and the 5th above it –

3rd  5th

Triads can be built on each degree of the major and minor scales, e.g. in C major –

They take their names from the degrees of the scale on which they are based: the triad on the tonic (key-note) is the 'tonic triad'; the triad on the dominant is the 'dominant triad'; and so on. As a shorthand device they are also referred to by roman numerals: I, II, III, IV, VI, VII for tonic, supertonic, mediant etc. The triads on I, IV and V are known as the 'primary' triads because, as will be explained in the next chapter, the chords derived from them have a particular importance.

Triads are classified as major, minor, augmented or diminished. A major triad consists of a major 3rd and a perfect 5th; a minor triad of a minor 3rd and a perfect 5th; a diminished triad of a minor 3rd and a diminished 5th; and an augmented triad of a major 3rd and an augmented 5th. From the last music example above it can be seen that in a major key the triads on I, IV and V are major; those on II, III and VI are minor; while the triad on VII is diminished.

In a minor key the tonic triad (I) is always minor, but triads on all the other degrees of the scale are variable because of the alternative forms of the 6th and

7th degrees derived from the harmonic and melodic scales. Thus the key of C minor produces the following triads –

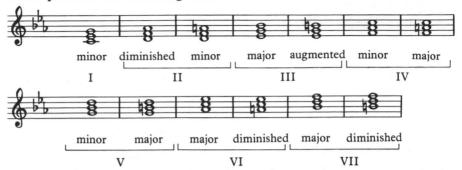

        minor   diminished   minor   major   augmented   minor   major

            I   II   III   IV

        minor   major   major   diminished   major   diminished

              V   VI   VII

All the triads so far have been in 'root position', because the root is the bottom note in each case. But the notes of a triad can be re-arranged so that either the 3rd or the 5th is at the bottom –

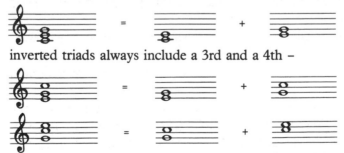

When the 3rd is at the bottom the triad is in the 'first inversion'; when the 5th is at the bottom it is in the 'second inversion'. This can be confusing. In the first and second inversions, '3rd' and '5th' continue to refer to the intervals from the root in the root-position triad: they do not refer to degrees of the scale, or to the intervals from the note which is actually at the bottom of an inverted triad. Indeed, it is worth noticing that, although triads in root position always consist of two intervals of a third,

inverted triads always include a 3rd and a 4th –

When Roman numerals are used to denote triads, the small letters 'a', 'b' and 'c' may be added to indicate 'root position', 'first inversion' and 'second inversion' respectively. Thus 'Vb', for example, means the first inversion of the dominant triad, and 'IVc' means the second inversion of the subdominant triad.

If a triad is arranged with all its notes as close to each other as possible –

it is said to be in 'close position'. If, however, the notes are spaced out in this fashion –

the triad is in 'open position'. An open-position triad is still described as being in root position, or in first or second inversion, according to which of its notes is at the bottom.

8/2 Chords

A triad is the simplest type of **chord**. The word 'chord' itself does not have a very precise meaning: it could be defined as 'three or more notes sounded together', but there is no limit to the number of notes in a chord (apart from practical considerations, e.g. a pianist has only ten fingers!). Over several centuries Western music gradually evolved an elaborate system of chords and their relationship to each other. In the hands of many composers this system began to be superseded around the beginning of the 20th century, as will be seen in Part II, Chapter 24. Nevertheless it is still in use, especially in 'popular' music, and it continues to form the basis of our musical experience.

The phrase used above – chords *and their relationship to each other* – cannot be too strongly emphasised. What is important about chords is the way they lead to and away from each other: they are not isolated events. However, this aspect of the matter will be considered in later chapters (see Chapter 9 and, in Part II, Chapters 16–17). What must first be explained here is the way in which the basic chords of diatonic music are constructed, the terms which are used to describe them, and the symbols which are used to represent them.

We have already seen the three notes of the triad arranged in two different ways: in close and in open position. In other arrangements they are called 'chords'. Such arrangements do not apply only to the repositioning of the three notes: they can also apply (and usually do) to the repetition of one or more of the three notes at different pitches. For example, the tonic triad of C major can produce all these chords –

– and many more besides. They all, however, consist of the notes C-E-G.

These particular chords have been laid out so that they can be played on the piano, but naturally the layout of a chord is affected by the instrument (or instruments or voices) which are going to perform it. A chord derived

from the dominant triad in A minor –  – could be arranged

for guitar in ways such as these –

but for a choir consisting of sopranos, altos, tenors and basses in ways such as these –

(Further information about the layout of music for vocal groups is given in Part II, Chapter 14.)

Chords are identified in exactly the same way as triads: a chord made up from the notes of a tonic triad is therefore a tonic chord, one made up from the notes of a dominant triad is a dominant chord, and so on. Similarly, if the root of the triad from which a chord is derived is at the bottom (= 'in the bass'), it will be a root-position chord; if the 3rd is in the bass, it will be a first-inversion chord; and if the 5th is in the bass, it will be a second-inversion chord. Chords can also be represented by the same symbols as triads: I, II, III etc., and a, b, c. Finally, they are major/minor/augmented/diminished like their corresponding triads.

All this can be illustrated by a detailed description of a few examples –

is the root position of a major chord: Va in G minor

is the first inversion of a minor chord: it could be either VIb in E major or Ib in C♯ minor

is the first inversion of a diminished chord: it could be either VIIb in E♭ major or IIb in C minor

is the first inversion of an augmented chord: IIIb in D minor

is the second inversion of a major chord: Ic in D major

More elaborate chords can be devised using not only the 3rd and 5th from the root but also the 7th, e.g. in C major –

They are called '7th' chords: 'tonic 7th' (shown as I⁷), 'supertonic 7th' (II⁷) and so on. (The 9th, 11th and 13th are used too: they will be discussed in Part II, Chapter 16/5.) By far the most common 7th chord is that of the dominant – the 'dominant 7th' (V⁷). Since a 7th chord is made out of four notes, there are *three* inversions in addition to the root position. The third inversion is indicated by the small letter 'd'. The following examples illustrate this. Again, notes may be used more than once in a chord –

As these examples show, in minor keys the 3rd above the root of the dominant 7th chord (i.e. the leading note) is always raised a semitone.

8/3 Chord notation in jazz etc.

The symbols we have used so far (I, IIb, V⁷ etc.) were designed for study purposes and are not used in performance. Two shorthand ways of indicating chords did, however, arise out of the practical needs of performers. The first is the chord notation used in jazz and other forms of 'popular' music. The second is much older: the 'figured bass' system used in music of the baroque period (roughly from the beginning of the 17th century to the middle of the 18th century). Both of these methods indicate the essential notes of chords while leaving the performer free to improvise the layout and, perhaps, the decoration of the chords.

The basic harmonies used in jazz are generally very simple. When complexities do occur, they are usually the result of an *improvised* decoration or elaboration of what are basically simple chord patterns. Since any such complexities are improvised, all the notation needs to show is the essential notes of the chords around which the performer is free to improvise. Jazz chord notation does not, therefore, need to be very detailed or complicated; nor is it. The letter name of the root of the chord is shown as a capital letter; and from this the 3rd and 5th can easily be deduced. The chord is assumed to be major unless shown otherwise: 'm' after the letter-name signifies a chord made out of the notes of the minor triad; '+' means that the triad is augmented; and 'o' means that it is diminished –

C   Cm   C+   Co

(Sometimes 'aug.' and 'dim.' are written instead of + and o.)

Any figures which are added represent intervals from the bass: C⁶ is a chord consisting of the notes of the C major triad (C E G) plus the 6th from C (A) –

C⁶

A figure ⁷ by itself implies the addition of a *minor* 7th –

C⁷

If the major 7th were required, the chord would be written 'C maj⁷' –

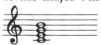

Cmaj⁷

(Note that here 'maj' refers to the ⁷ and not to the C.)

None of the above symbols, however, demands that the root of the chord has to be in the bass: normally any of the notes may be the bass note, at the choice of the performer. On the rare occasions when the bass note is specified, its letter name is given after an oblique stroke (/) following the chord description, e.g. Cm/G, implying –

Sometimes this may be found written as 'Cm (G bass)' or as 'C mi (root G)', although the latter is thoroughly confusing since this is not the standard meaning of 'root'.

It cannot be too strongly emphasised that jazz chord notation shows only the bare outlines of the harmony. A great deal of latitude is left to the performer, who may freely decorate the given chords or enrich them with additional notes as the spirit moves.

8/4 Figured bass

Usually all baroque music, except that for a solo player, included a part for a **continuo** instrument. The continuo could be any instrument which produced chords, though normally either the harpsichord or the organ was used. It was the job of the continuo player to ensure that the required harmonies were complete and clear. If essential harmony notes were missing from other parts, they would be provided by the continuo. Sometimes, indeed, the other parts were just a solo melody and a bass instrument – perhaps just the bass instrument – and then the entire responsibility for supplying complete chords fell upon the continuo player. The music actually played consisted of the bass line (as performed, for example, by cellos and double basses in an orchestra), underneath which were written figures. These figures represented the intervals above the note, and the required chord was made out of these notes. For example, means that the chord is constructed from the bass note (C), the 3rd above it (E) and the 5th above it (G). It could be laid out in any way the performer pleased, e.g. –

All $^5_3$ chords are root-position chords. The figures for a first inversion are $^6_3$,

e.g.  . Here the chord is to be constructed out of the bass note (E),

the 3rd above it (G) and the 6th above it (C). Again it is up to the performer how the notes are to be distributed: these are just a few possibilities –

A second-inversion chord is shown by the figures $^6_4$ below the bass note.

Thus  implies the notes A, D (the 4th) and F♯ (the 6th) – F *sharp*

because of the key signature. Here are a few of the many ways in which it can be 'realised' (this is the term used to denote the way in which a figured bass is actually performed) –

Some other points which should be mentioned in this introduction to figured bass are:

(i) An accidental placed immediately next to a figure (either before or after)
it) refers to the note it represents. Thus ⟨figure⟩ means a chord

consisting of the notes G, C and E *natural* (in spite of the key signature).[1]

(ii) The $^5_3$ is usually omitted under root-position chords: a bass note without figures is understood to be a $^5_3$ (root-position) chord. An accidental by itself under a note, e.g. ⟨figure⟩ , applies to the 3rd of a $^5_3$ chord (thus, in this case, E-G *sharp*-B).

(iii) $^6_3$ chords are usually represented by just the figure 6, e.g. ⟨figure⟩ ,

---

[1] In the baroque period, a stroke through a figure (2, 4, 3, 6, 7 or 7) was often used to indicate a note *raised* by a chromatic semitone. It should also be noted that baroque composers did not always figure the bass fully: often they only put in figures here and there, where they thought the continuo player might not *guess* what was wanted. In such circumstances, a chord without figures would not necessarily be a $^5_3$ chord.

meaning Eb–G–C. If the 3rd has to be chromatically altered, it is shown by the appropriate accidental *underneath* the 6. Hence  implies a

chord of Eb, Gb and C. If the C were to be flattened as well the figuring would become ⟨figure⟩ .

(iv) The full figuring for a 7th chord and its inversions would be: $\frac{7}{5}$ (root position), $\frac{6}{5}$ (first inversion), $\frac{6}{4}$ (second inversion), and $\frac{6}{4}$ (third inversion). In practice, these are generally contracted to 7, $\frac{6}{5}$, $\frac{4}{3}$ and $\frac{4}{2}$, unless they have to be written out more fully so that any necessary accidentals can be shown. These points can be illustrated by the following, which represent the figured-bass notation of the dominant 7th chords at the bottom of p.61 –

Some writers on music combine figured-bass symbols with the Roman-figure chord symbols explained earlier: thus I $\frac{6}{3}$ rather than Ib may be used for the first inversion of a tonic chord, or V $\frac{6}{4}$ rather than Vc for the second inversion of a dominant chord (see Part II, Appendix D).

8/5 Chord layouts

On instruments which can play chords – the piano is the most obvious example – chords are frequently played not with all the notes sounding together simultaneously but with them broken up in various patterns. J. S. Bach's first Prelude in the '48' (in C major), for example, begins –

The passage on the previous page is just an elaboration of –

In figured-bass notation it could be represented thus –

Chords arranged as successions of notes in this way (with or without repetitions) are called **broken chords**. One particular form was much used in the left-hand part of 18th-century keyboard music, e.g. –

Mozart, Piano Sonata in C, K.545 (1st mvt)

where the music on the lower stave is merely an elaboration of

This type of figuration is known as an **Alberti bass**, after the Italian composer, Domenico Alberti, who popularised it.

A chord arranged with all its notes in ascending or descending order is an **arpeggio** (from the Italian word for 'harp', an instrument which is particularly well adapted to this kind of playing). These, for example, are two-octave arpeggios of the chord of C major –

CHAPTER 9

Phrases and Cadences

9/1 The phrase

The way in which words are grouped together to make phrases, sentences and paragraphs is paralleled in music. In fact all three words – **phrase, sentence** and **paragraph** – are also used in analysing music: phrases are grouped together to form musical sentences, and sentences are grouped together to form musical paragraphs. Already this is beginning to take us into the study of musical form which is not the subject of this book. Nevertheless, something must be said about the simplest of these groupings – the phrase – because of its intrinsic musical importance and because it is associated with other basic features such as cadences.

'Phrase' is defined in *Chambers 20th Century Dictionary* as 'a group of words . . . felt as expressing a single idea or constituting a single element in the sentence', and in its musical sense as 'a short group of notes felt to form a unit'. A simple example might be –

Traditional, 'Twinkle, twinkle, little star'

There are no hard-and-fast rules about phrases – 'felt' is an important word in both the dictionary definitions above – and musicians do not invariably agree about the phrasing of a piece. Some might argue that the example above consists of *two* phrases: bars 1–4 and 5–8, indicated by ⌐‐‐‐‐‐¬ marks here –

(⌐‐‐‐‐‐‐¬ markings are a convenient method of indicating phrase lengths *for study purposes* and will be used for this purpose again in later examples in this chapter. They are used here to prevent confusion with the phrasing marks or articulation marks which are used in music intended for actual performance. Since the latter often show a good deal more than the mere beginnings and endings of phrases, they are necessarily more subtle and detailed. This aspect of the matter will be explained in Chapter 11.)

When verses are set to music, the phrases often coincide with the lines (or with pairs of lines) of the verses. This is nearly always true in simple forms such as hymns, carols, nursery songs, folksongs and the like, e.g. –

As sweet Polly Oliver lay musing in bed,
A sudden, strange fancy came into her head;
'Nor father nor mother shall make me false prove!
I'll 'list [enlist] for a soldier and follow my love!'

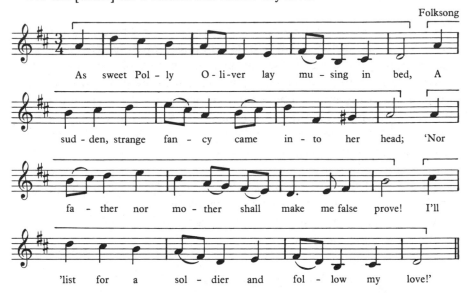

In such cases the phrases are often of the same length, usually two or (as in the last example) four bars. A consequence of this is that the beginnings and endings of phrases normally complement each other: e.g. if a phrase in $\frac{3}{4}$ starts on the third beat of a bar (as above), it must end with the second (as on 'bed', 'head' and 'prove') so that the next phrase can also begin on the third. Similarly, if the same music is repeated for another verse of the words, the first verse will have to end with the second beat so that the next verse can begin again on the third –

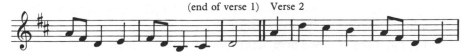

Much music which is purely instrumental has this kind of regular phrasing too – particularly shorter pieces such as dances, marches etc. An example is the *Gavotta* in Prokofiev's *Classical Symphony*, the opening of which is shown below. To indicate the phrase structure, ⌐‾‾‾¬ marks have again been added. (Directions concerning repeats and violin bowing, which will be explained in Chapters 13 and 19, Part II, respectively, have been omitted.)

In such cases, the convention about balancing an incomplete opening bar with an incomplete bar at the end (the two adding up to one complete bar) is generally observed. A piece which starts $\frac{3}{4}$ ♪ |, for example, will finish with a bar containing the equivalent of 2½ crotchets, e.g. ♩ ♪ ‖ or ♩ 𝄽 ⁊ ‖ etc. However, this convention is not always followed nowadays, and in longer pieces (such as the first movement of a sonata) it has never been very consistently observed.

A weak-beat opening to a phrase (as in 'Sweet Polly Oliver' and in the Prokofiev *Gavotta* above) is called an **anacrusis** – a term also used in poetry.

9/2 Cadences

9/2a Cadence and phrase

The end of a phrase is a point of rest or relaxation in the music: it is called a **cadence** (from the Latin word meaning 'to fall'). The most complete point of rest is obviously the end of the last phrase in a piece, since the music then stops altogether; but the end of each intermediate phrase also has a feeling of relaxation. It is a sort of breathing space – for wind players and singers, indeed, it almost always *is* a breathing space. Something has finished; something else is about to begin.

Cadences are not just a matter of melody: chords also are involved. The particular chords used contribute towards the feeling of relaxation and make it more or less definite. Indeed, cadences are categorised according to the chords involved, as we are about to see. But first it must be emphasised that the use of particular chords does not in itself produce a cadence. The chords must be used at the right time, i.e. at the end of a phrase: they reinforce the feeling of relaxation already given to the music by the rhythm and the melodic shape.

Virtually without exception, tonal music ends on the tonic chord. There is a reason for this. As was explained in Chapters 2 and 4, the pitches of the notes from which a piece is made can be represented as a scale based on the tonic, to which all the other notes are related (see especially 4/4). The tonic note is the foundation of the whole thing. Consequently, the root-position chord built upon it – the tonic chord – is the most stable of all chords: all other chords lead to *it*. It is often compared to home: if one thinks of listening to a piece of music as a kind of musical journey, the final tonic chord is the point at which one arrives home again.

Cadences which end on the tonic chord, therefore, have a particularly 'final' feeling. Although they are used not only at the end of a piece, there is always a possibility that, if they are used in the middle, they may make it sound as though it has come to a premature halt. Thus it is useful to distinguish between cadences which end with the tonic chord and those which do not: those which *can* end a piece (even though they are sometimes used in the middle too) and those which are never used at the end. Four types of cadence are especially common and have been given individual names: two which end on the tonic chord – the perfect cadence (or full close) and the plagal cadence; and two which are used only at intermediate points – the imperfect cadence (or half close) and the interrupted cadence.

9/2b Perfect cadence

The chord which most powerfully leads to the tonic chord is the dominant chord, and the progression from a dominant to a tonic chord at a phrase ending forms the **perfect cadence**. One of the reasons for the dominant chord's special power is to be found in acoustical considerations – the 5th being the next harmonic after the fundamental note and its octave – and need not detain us here. But the other reason has to be emphasised: the presence in the chord of the leading note of the scale. It is a fact of melody that the leading note, as its name implies, has a tendency to move up a semitone to the tonic. Consequently, the essential elements in a perfect cadence are a move from the dominant to the tonic in the bass, and above the bass a move from the leading note to the tonic, e.g. in C major and C minor –

The move from leading note to tonic can be at the top or in the middle of the chords, although the feeling of finality is stronger when the music ends with the tonic in the melody as well as in the bass. These are typical perfect cadences laid out for keyboard in the key of G major –

The dominant 7th chord (the dominant chord containing also the 7th from the root) prepares the tonic even more powerfully because of the need for the dissonant interval of the 7th to be resolved (see 7/5). Thus in a dominant 7th to tonic progression the essential elements in the perfect cadence become –

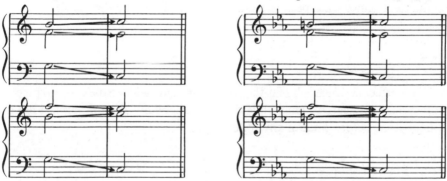

The following examples, also for keyboard, show typical uses in various keys –

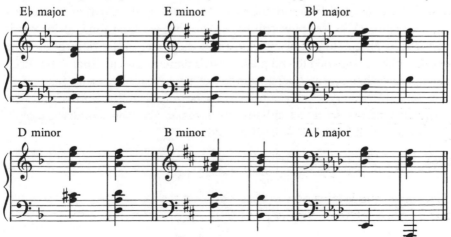

Either or both of the two chords may be inverted, e.g. in C major–

Vb   V⁷b   Ib   V⁷d   Ib

although at a *final* cadence the tonic is always in root position. The progression VIIb-I is very similar in effect to V⁷c-I and can be regarded as a type of perfect cadence.

Compare 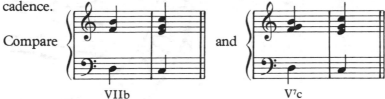 and

VIIb   V⁷c

Both are relatively weak as *final* cadences, since the effect of the bass is more powerful if it moves not by a single step but by a jump from the root of V –

    The perfect cadence is by far the most common cadence used to end pieces; in fact one may search a long while through a book of songs or hymn tunes or sonatas etc., before finding any other.

9/2c Plagal cadence

The **plagal cadence** consists of the subdominant chord followed by the tonic chord. Its effect as a final cadence is less compelling than that of the perfect cadence since IV is less powerful than V as a preparation for I, lacking as it does the leading note with its push towards the tonic. In the 16th century the plagal cadence was used to end pieces much more frequently than it has been since. Nevertheless, some later composers have been especially fond of it, e.g. Sibelius: a very clear example is to be found at the end of the first movement of his Third Symphony (in C major). A more familiar example occurs at the end of *Good King Wenceslas* –

IV   I

9/2d Imperfect cadence

The dominant chord itself can make a *temporary* resting-place, and a cadence ending on the dominant is called an **imperfect cadence**. Various chords can be used to precede the dominant: I, II, IV and VI are all common. These two imperfect cadences at the opening of the second movement of Beethoven's Piano Sonata, Op.14 No.2, are typical –

9/2e Interrupted cadence

The **interrupted cadence**, which might be better called the 'interrupted perfect cadence', occurs where a dominant chord leads the listener to expect a tonic chord (and hence a perfect cadence) but is in fact followed by any chord *except* the tonic. There is a splendid example near the end of Bach's harmonisation of a chorale usually sung to the English words, 'Sleepers wake' or 'Wake, O wake' –

J. S. Bach, *Wachet Auf*

9/2f Other cadences

Perfect, plagal, imperfect and interrupted cadences are the most common, but there are others: e.g. the VI-IV cadence, here shown at the end of the second line of Parry's *Jerusalem* –

etc.

VI   IV

9/2g Feminine endings

More often than not, the last chord of any cadence occurs on a stronger beat than the first. But when the second chord is *less* strongly accented, the phrase is said to have a **feminine ending**, or the cadence itself is described as 'feminine'. The perfect cadence in bar 4 of the Schumann passage quoted on p.81 is an example. An imperfect cadence, with Ic-V used as a feminine ending, was almost a hallmark of music of the classical period (*c.*1770–1830), as in the last bar of this extract from a chorus in Haydn's oratorio, *The Creation* –

The   hea - vens are   tel - ling the   glo -   ry   of   God ____

CHAPTER 10

Tempo, Dynamics and Mood

Music notation was at first concerned only with the barest facts: the pitches of the notes and their duration, later with time signatures and key signatures. Even J. S. Bach very rarely gave any instructions about speed, or about softness and loudness (dynamics), or about how notes are to be grouped into phrases or smaller units (phrasing or articulation). These things could sometimes be deduced from the character of the music – people were more or less agreed about suitable speeds for different types of dances, for example – but a great deal was left to the performer to decide. However, by the time Bach died in 1750 he had become distinctly old-fashioned in this respect. Indeed, from the late 17th century onwards composers became more and more concerned to show as precisely as possible how they wanted their music performed, until by the early 20th century very meticulous directions were given, and the freedom of performers to decide things for themselves was vastly reduced.

Good performers, it should be said, do not resent this. After all, they are seeking to turn into real sounds the music which the composer had in his imagination; the more they can discover what exactly he had in mind, the more they are helped. And they are still left with important responsibilities of judgement. What is 'loud' in a concert hall, for example, will be far *too* loud in a small room; a contrast of speed or a balance between melody and accompaniment, which might be right in some circumstances, might not be satisfactory in others, and so on. Music can never be written down so exactly and in such detail that performers become simply mechanics: always their artistic sensibilities are demanded.

10/1 Tempo

It was explained in 1/3 that there are two ways of specifying the speed at the beginning of a piece: either a metronome mark or a direction in words. Metronome marks are sometimes written with '*c.*' (for *circa* = 'about') in front of the figure, e.g. $\bmJ$ = *c*.112. Probably no composer ever expects his metronome speeds to be observed absolutely exactly, and speeds may have to be modified slightly in the light of practical circumstances, such as a performance in a very resonant building. Nevertheless, metronome marks are the clearest possible indications of tempo and must always be taken seriously: to play a piece very much faster or slower than a given metronome mark misrepresents what a composer wants.[1] One trap people sometimes fall into is to misread not the figure but the note value: e.g. $\sbond = 60$ might be misread as $\sbond = 60$, resulting in a performance at only half speed.

Directions in words do not pretend to be as precise as metronome marks, and they have other pitfalls. The most obvious is that they may be written in a language which the performer does not understand (see the Glossary of Foreign Words used for Performance Directions). Fortunately, Italian was for so long the international language of music that all the words it commonly used for music – e.g. *adagio, andante, allegro* etc. – are universally understood by musicians and are still universally used. Today, English is probably the nearest thing there is to an international language, but English-speaking composers also tend to follow the convention of using Italian terms for speed and other directions.

Another pitfall is that, even assuming the words are understood, they may be exaggerated. *Allegro*, for example, might reasonably be interpreted as 'quick', but it does not mean '*very* quick', still less 'as quickly as possible'. Words which denote gradual changes of speed are often exaggerated or distorted. *Accelerando* (abbreviated as *accel.*), for example, means 'gradually getting faster' not 'suddenly faster': the listener should only gradually become aware that the music is speeding up. Similarly, *rallentando* (*rall.*) and *ritardando* (*rit.* or *ritard.*) imply a gradual slowing down, not an abrupt change of speed.

Yet another pitfall is that words sometimes gradually change their meaning over the centuries. *Allegro*, for example, was originally used to describe not so much speed as a mood: 'cheerful' or 'lively' (the literal meaning of the word). *Largo*, which is usually thought of as implying a very slow tempo, was described by Henry Purcell (in the Preface to his *Sonatas of III Parts*, 1683) as a 'middle movement', meaning a medium speed. *Ritenuto* (*rit.* or *riten.*) is another case in point: literally it means 'held back' and thus a sudden change to a slower tempo, but it is now generally used in the same sense as *rallentando* and *ritardando*, i.e. a gradual slowing down, though possibly a more marked slowing down than the other words imply. Indeed, *rit.* is used as an abbreviation for both *ritenuto* and *ritardando*: it might be logical but it would also be unrealistically pedantic to suggest that it should be reserved for one or the other, or that *ritenuto* can only mean a sudden slowing down. Incidentally, any speeding-up or slowing-down direction remains in force until a new tempo direction – or *a tempo* (= 'in time') – is reached, although composers do not always remember this.

[1]A metronome mark printed within square brackets is the tempo recommended by an editor and does not necessarily represent the composer's intention. For an interesting analysis of conflicting metronome marks in a particular work, see Howard Ferguson's introduction to the Associated Board edition of Schumann's *Kinderscenen*, Op.15.

There is a particular device of notation which can occur at changes of time signature, e.g. –

♩. = ♩ here means that the crotchet beats in ¾ have exactly the same duration as the dotted crotchet beats in ⅜. This type of direction is perfectly clear if written as above, with the = over the bar-line, the old note value to the left of it and the new one to the right. Unfortunately, the whole formula used to be placed after the change of time signature, with no consistency about which note value relates to which time signature. This, for example, is ambiguous –

It probably indicates that a minim in 4/4 = a crotchet in 2/4, but it could be understood to mean that a crotchet in 4/4 = a minim in 2/4. Fortunately, a study of the context combined with a little common sense usually clarifies what is wanted, but the notation of the previous example precludes confusion and should be regarded as standard.

The sign called a **fermata** – ⌢ above (or ⌣ below) a note or rest – is now the standard indication of a pause[1]. How long a pause is a matter of discretion, but again there is a danger of exaggeration: if a composer wants a long pause he generally writes *lunga pausa* as well. 'G.P.' (= general pause) added to a pause mark over a rest is a sign only used when a group of players (as in an orchestra) is involved: it warns them that they are all silent at the same time.

Sometimes a regular beat is abandoned altogether and note values have no precise significance. This happens particularly in florid passages (often joining sections) as in this example, near the end of Beethoven's Piano Sonata in E♭, Op.27 No.1 –

(The signs under the last three notes are explained in 11/3.)

---

[1] In baroque and earlier music, however, the sign was commonly used merely to show an important structural point, e.g. the end of a section in the music. J. S. Bach, for example, marked the ends of the lines (phrases) of his chorales with a ⌢, implying a breath but not normally a halt in the movement.

This example is taken from a movement which is actually in $\frac{3}{4}$, and the bass stave conforms with this; nevertheless the treble stave does not. All that can be said is that after a pause on the first note there is a rapid run of notes, shown as one long group of semiquavers, followed by three much slower notes at a free tempo. Runs like this are usually printed in small type (as here), though it is perhaps more common for them to be written as demisemiquavers rather than semiquavers. There are also some word directions which free the performer from a strict beat, such as *ad libitum* (*ad lib.*), 'at discretion', and *senza misura*, 'without measure'.

Another word which gives the performer some rhythmic freedom is *rubato* (literally meaning 'robbed', as in *tempo rubato*). This can have two, somewhat different, interpretations. In the first, the underlying pulse of the music as a whole becomes slightly flexible. In the second, the accompaniment remains in strict time but the melody is flexible: a technique which jazz soloists, playing or singing with some freedom against a strict-time backing, have made familiar. This, however, was not a 20th-century innovation. Both Mozart and Chopin, for example, used what is essentially the same technique in playing the piano when they accompanied an expressive, 'singing' melody in the right hand with a left hand in strict time.

10/2 Dynamics

Word directions concerning softness and loudness are nowadays always written as abbreviations, e.g. *f* for *forte* (loud), *mf* for *mezzo-forte* (medium – literally 'half' – loud), *p* for *piano* (soft), *mp* for *mezzo-piano* (medium soft). Very loud is written as *ff* (for *fortissimo*), and very soft as *pp* (*pianissimo*). Thereafter composers sometimes get carried away and go on adding *f*s and *p*s regardless – *fff*, *pppp* etc. There is rarely much real meaning in going beyond three *f*s or *p*s, however: when Tchaikovsky marked a bassoon solo *pppppp* in the first movement of his 6th Symphony, he certainly ensured that the player would not miss the fact that the passage was to be played very softly indeed, but it is difficult to see what precise difference one *p* more or less would have made.

But if composers sometimes exaggerate, so too do performers: *f* should not be interpreted as 'as loud as possible' nor *p* as 'practically inaudible'! Dynamic marks can never be *exact* indications of the volume of sound needed: they always have to be assessed in relation to other dynamic marks in the piece, and to the mood of the music as a whole – and also to its style and historical period. A late sonata by Beethoven, for example, can be expected to have a wider dynamic range and more extreme contrasts than a sonata by, say, Mozart.

The full name for the piano (the instrument) is of course 'pianoforte', sometimes abbreviated to 'pf'; but *pf* used as a dynamic mark means *poco forte* (slightly loud). However, the reverse, *fp* – which is much more common – means *forte piano*: loud and then immediately soft. Rather similar are the directions *sforzato* and *sforzando* (both abbreviated as either *sf* or *sfz*), literally meaning 'forced' and 'forcing' – in effect a sudden accent applied to an individual note or chord. *Rinforzato* and *rinforzando* (*rf*, *rfz* or *rinf.*), literally 'reinforced' and 'reinforcing', are often used with the same meaning, though they may imply a sudden growth in volume (perhaps applied to a short group of notes) or that a part is to stand out prominently.

Accentuation can also be shown by the signs >, written above or below a note or chord, and ∧ written above or ∨ written below. Often no very clear distinction is made between them but, when it is, ∧ and ∨ are stronger than > (< is never used.) Accent marks are used in soft music as well as in loud and must always be scaled according to the context: > occurring in a soft passage, for example, certainly does not imply a violent explosion. (Two other signs involving emphasis will be discussed in 11/3.)

Gradual changes of dynamic level can be shown by words or signs. *Crescendo* (usually written in abbreviated form as *cresc.*) means 'getting louder'. *Diminuendo* (*dim.* or *dimin.*) and *decrescendo* (*decresc.*) both mean 'getting softer', though the former is the more usual term. Sometimes these words are spaced out, e.g. *cre* – – – *scen* – – – *do*. This can be a useful reminder to the performer but is not strictly necessary: even in an abbreviated form (e.g. *cresc.*) the direction always continues in force until a new dynamic level is reached.

Unfortunately, composers sometimes forget to show where the dynamic change ends. This is not a problem if signs are used instead of words: —————————— for 'getting louder' and —————— for 'getting softer'. (Musicians often call these signs 'hairpins'.) Both have a clear beginning and ending although, unless a dynamic mark is put at the end, it is still not clear just how *much* louder or softer the music becomes. *p* ————— by itself, for example, could imply *p* ————— *mf* or *p* ————— *fff* . It is not practicable to draw ————— and ————— signs over more than a few bars, whereas word directions can remain in force for pages if necessary.

Gradual changes of dynamic level can be qualified by words such as *poco a poco* (little by little) and *molto* (much). But with or without these qualifications, and however they are notated, they need careful and even grading. This is particularly important where they begin: as with gradual changes of speed the listener should not become instantly aware that a change is taking place.

10/3 Mood

Word directions are often given to describe the general mood or character of
the music: words such as *risoluto* (resolute), *mesto* (sad), *giocoso* (playful) and
tranquillo (peaceful). Invariably such directions have implications concerning
tempo or dynamics or phrasing (see the following chapter), or possibly all of
these. It would clearly be inappropriate to play a piece marked *tranquillo* very
fast or very loud or in a very jerky way.

Many such word directions are listed in the Glossary of Foreign Words
used for Performance Directions where their meanings are given.

CHAPTER 11

Articulation

11/1 Phrasing marks

The fact that the notes forming a phrase are 'felt to form a unit' (see 9/1) does not mean that they cannot be separated from each other. Phrases are often subdivided into smaller groups of notes with tiny gaps between them; some or all of the notes may be subdivided by means of signs to be explained shortly; and phrases may even include rests, e.g. –

Schumann, 'Soldier's March' (*Album for the Young*)

Here there are two phrases: bars 1–4 and 5–8. Although there are no marks to show the phrase structure, several factors make it clear to the listener, such as the repetition of bars 1 and 2 in bars 5 and 6, the rhythmic repetition of bars 1–4 in bars 5–8, and the perfect cadences in bars 4 and 8 (in G and D major respectively). A similar example is the passage by Beethoven quoted on p.73.

When composers use what are often loosely called 'phrasing marks', they generally show a good deal more than where phrases begin and end. They are more concerned to indicate in detail how the notes within a phrase are to be *performed*: whether they are to be separated from each other, whether they are to be played smoothly in groups of two or more, and so on. Often, indeed, composers' directions are precise playing instructions designed specifically for particular instruments, such as bowing marks for strings. Signs giving technical directions of this kind will be explained when individual instruments are discussed in Chapters 19–21 in Part II. Meanwhile, this chapter will be concerned with directions which have a general application to all performers.

11/2 The slur

Signs showing whether notes are to be separated or grouped together are most accurately described as **articulation** marks. The only circumstance in which an articulation mark also coincides with a complete phrase (and might thus be literally called a 'phrase mark') is when a curved line called a **slur** stretches from the first note of the phrase to the last, e.g. –

Debussy, 'Hommage à Rameau' (*Images*)

Used in this way, the slur means that all the notes within it are to be played smoothly (*legato*), without any breaks between them. (A short vertical stroke through the middle of a slur ⌐ merely indicates that the slur has been added by an editor. Small brackets either side of a slur (⌐) or a broken slur ⌐ are other ways of denoting the same thing.)

A slur has exactly the same meaning when it embraces a smaller group of notes, e.g. –

Bartók, *For Children*, Vol.I No.3

In performance, the end of a slur implies a slight shortening of its last note, with a brief silence before the next note. Thus, the melody of the example above would be played approximately

(There is no need to shorten the left-hand minims since they are already followed by silences – both have rests after them.)

The small break in sound implied by consecutive slurs, e.g. –

is sometimes shown instead by a comma above the stave –

Although they look the same, a slur linking two different notes (e.g.) should not of course be confused with a tie, where the curved line joins two notes of the same pitch (e.g.) to produce one extended sound.

The smooth linking of notes is sometimes implied by unconventional beaming. An example occurs at the opening of Beethoven's Piano Sonata in D, Op.10 No.3, where, contrary to normal procedure, notes are beamed together across bar-lines –

Although Beethoven here uses slurs as well, the beaming makes clear his intentions even more compellingly than slurs alone would have done. Beaming like this became more common during the 19th century, though often with additional implications concerning accentuation and rhythmic grouping.

For the use of the slur in connection with triplets and word underlay, see 3/3 and 6/1 respectively. Its special meaning for string and wind players will be explained in Part II, 19/2 and 20/6 respectively.

11/3 Staccato signs

Several signs are used to show that a note is to be shortened. The most common is the **staccato** dot, normally positioned above or below the note-head: . Where there are two parts on a stave, the dot is positioned by the appropriate stem:

Just how much a note is to be shortened will depend upon its value and upon the tempo. This, for example,

at a slow speed might be played

but at a quicker speed (where there is less time to hold the notes) might become

Staccato dots, therefore, do *not* mean that the notes are to be made as short as possible. Indeed, their effect can be modified further when two or more staccato dots are linked by a slur. Thus, if

were to be performed

the following variations at the same speed might be played as shown –

As can be seen above, two staccato notes of the same pitch linked by a slur are not *tied* notes. A more ambiguous situation arises if only the second note has a staccato dot, e.g. ![notation]. String players will readily understand this as two *separate* notes played in one bow; pianists and others should also reiterate the second note. If, however, the dot is placed outside the slur, ![notation], the implication is that the notes are tied, i.e. the second note is not reiterated, though shortened in value.

The use of a dot to indicate a staccato note was not introduced until the latter part of the 18th century. Earlier a short stroke (♩) or a wedge-shaped sign (♩) was used for the same purpose. Eventually the wedge became the standard direction that a note is to be played as briefly as possible (*staccatissimo*), whatever its written value or the tempo. But it often appears to suggest an accent too: indeed, Mozart sometimes (not always) used it to show an accent without shortening.

The opposite of staccato may be shown by the word *tenuto* (often abbreviated to *ten.*). Any notes to which this direction applies are to be held for their full value and not shortened in any way. (In some circumstances, *tenuto* may even imply a slight lengthening, occasionally even a short pause: these, however, are not the normal implications of the term.) A horizontal dash above or below a note (♩) may also indicate *tenuto* (and hence it is sometimes called a 'tenuto mark'), although this sign has come to be used primarily as an indication of pressure or emphasis – which, in practice, entails a slight degree of separation between notes so marked. Consequently, ♩ ♩ is similar to ♩ ♩ but rather weightier. Slurring notes with horizontal dashes (♩ ♩) may indicate a somewhat smaller separation, but in practice the slur makes little difference – except to string players, to whom it is a bowing direction (see 19/2). On the other hand, the combination of staccato dots with horizontal dashes (♩ ♩) increases the separation or, to put it the other way round, gives more emphasis to a note marked with a staccato dot.

11/4 Double phrasing

Extended slurs are sometimes superimposed over groups of notes which are already articulated by subsidiary slurs and/or by staccato dots and other separation signs, and even by rests, e.g. –

(Agitato, ma non troppo presto)   Brahms, *Capriccio*, Op.76 No.5

A superimposed slur shows that the notes within it still belong to each other as a group, in spite of the small breaks in sound between some of them. Thus, when the above passage is played, it must convey the feeling that it consists of

---

[1] In effect, the first three bars of the melody shown here are in $\frac{3}{4}$, but the piece as a whole is in $\frac{6}{8}$.

1 + 1 + 2 bars. The primary way of achieving this is to make relatively large breaks after the two A♯s, e.g. by playing each as a quaver followed by a quaver rest. In practice, other factors – often too subtle to be shown in notation – may also contribute to a musical and clear sense of phrasing: for example, small shadings and contrasts of dynamic levels, touches of rubato, and so on.

11/5 Textual and stylistic problems

Finally in this chapter, it has to be said that composers are not always careful in their use of phrasing marks. What appear to be inconsistencies, even mistakes, are not uncommon; and finding solutions to the performance problems which they raise can demand considerable thought and musicianship.

Moreover, conventions have changed over the years. For example, the use of long slurs to indicate an extended legato (as in the Debussy example on p.82) or a phrase length (such as the superimposed slur in the Brahms passage quoted above) originated only around the early 19th century – though it developed relentlessly thereafter. Composers of the classical period would usually have divided a legato phrase into smaller sections each with a separate slur, usually ending at the bar-line or before the last note, e.g. –

In such cases, a break in sound at the end of the slur was not necessarily intended – which is not to say that it is always inappropriate.[1]

The difficulties of interpreting music of the classical and earlier periods have been seriously compounded by many editors until quite recent times. Often they *altered* phrasing marks (and indeed other directions), substituting what they believed – not always correctly – to be implied by the original notation, or to be more appropriate to modern instruments. And where none existed in the original, they did not hesitate to add their own phrasing marks – inappropriate though these often were to the style of the music. In neither case was it revealed just what had been altered or added. Today's editors are usually more meticulous and will show as precisely as possible what the composer actually wrote, distinguishing clearly any additions or revisions suggested by the editor. This is not to guarantee, of course, that modern editions are invariably reliable, and it goes without saying that a bad edition, old or new, is no better for having been recently reprinted.

[1] For further information, see Howard Ferguson's *Keyboard Interpretation* (Oxford University Press, London 1975), specifically pp.64–5; and, in more detail, Chapter 3 of Eva and Paul Badura-Skoda's *Interpreting Mozart on the Keyboard* (Barrie & Rockliff, London 1962).

CHAPTER 12

Ornaments and Embellishments

One of the most familiar features of music today is the way in which jazz players improvise elaborate decorations to the melody. Although the style has changed, the principle itself is not new. In earlier centuries also, the improvisation of decorations was often regarded as an important part of a solo performer's skill. Far from objecting to this, composers (who were often performers too) wrote their music in the expectation that it would be decorated. A bare performance of the written notes, particularly of a slow melody, would have been thought very dull.

Various decorative patterns became standardised, and composers were able to indicate them by means of special symbols – a kind of musical shorthand. An absence of such symbols did not, however, mean that the music was to be performed without ornamentation. From about 1600 to the second half of the 18th century, an enormous number of different symbols were used, varying according to the period, to the locality, and even to the individual composer. Some composers (J. S. Bach among them) drew up lists of ornament symbols with explanations of how they were to be performed; and sometimes there are instruction books and other sources from the period which give guidance.

Nevertheless, these explanations do not always cover every circumstance. Nor is it always certain how far they applied to music of a slightly earlier or later date, or to music from a different region. Consequently, it is now often a difficult and controversial matter to decide exactly how to interpret a symbol written two centuries or more ago; and unless modern performers have made a special study of these problems, they are likely to need expert advice. Fortunately, modern editors of early music sometimes give this advice either in a preface or in the music itself (usually by writing out the ornament in full above the music text or by way of a footnote) or by translating an obsolete symbol into modern notation; but such advice, as most editors point out, cannot be definitive and usually represents no more than one of several ways of interpreting an ornament symbol.

From the latter part of the 18th century the use of ornament symbols gradually diminished: composers increasingly wrote out the music in full. Only a few symbols are still in regular use today, and these will be described first of all. Afterwards, some of the more common symbols from earlier periods will be considered.

12/1 Symbols still in regular use

12/1a Grace notes

Grace notes can be recognised by two features: (i) they are printed as small-size notes; (ii) they are disregarded so far as the rhythm of the full-size notes is concerned, i.e. the rhythm values 'add up' to a complete bar without them.

A single grace note is shown as a small-size quaver with a diagonal stroke through it – ♪ , usually joined by a tiny slur to the following full-size note (the principal note) – . This can be played in one of three ways:

(i)   just before the beat –

(ii) on the beat (but with the accent on the principal note)

(iii) *simultaneously* with the principal note (on the beat), but then immediately released

The first method is the most usual, or the third if the ♪ is used in a very rapid passage. But in practice it can be difficult or even impossible to distinguish between the three; and not all instruments *can* play two notes simultaneously. Whichever way it is performed, the ♪ is generally called an **acciaccatura**, although strictly speaking the term applies only to the third (simultaneous) method (the Italian word derives from a word meaning to 'bruise' or 'pound'; 'crushed note' is sometimes used as an English equivalent).

Groups of two or more grace notes are shown as quavers or, more often, notes of shorter value, beamed together. They are performed as quickly as possible, slipped in just before the following full-size note; though in a lyrical and expressive melody it may be appropriate to play them more deliberately.

What is not always certain is whether they should be played on the beat or before it: for example, whether the grace notes in the following passage should take their time from the F♯ before the bar-line or from the dotted quaver A after it. Which note in the melody coincides with the low A in the bass?

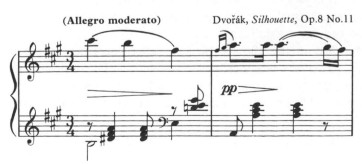

(**Allegro moderato**)   Dvořák, *Silhouette*, Op.8 No.11

During the 19th century it became increasingly common for composers to expect grace notes such as these to be placed before the beat (as seems the best solution here); and this is what is normally required in 20th-century music also. Nevertheless, it may not invariably be what is wanted. Fortunately, composers sometimes leave performers in no doubt about how grace notes are to be performed. In the following passage, for example, the clear implication of putting them before the bar-line is that they are to be performed before the beat –

(Andante tranquillo)   Ireland, *The Holy Boy*

while in the next one there is a verbal instruction that they are to be played on the beat –

Debussy, Preludes Bk.I: 'Minstrels'

Modéré

p les ''gruppetti'' sur le temps

In the 18th century (as we shall see shortly), it had been conventional for ornaments to be performed starting *on* the beat, and many composers continued this tradition into the first part of the 19th century. Chopin, for example, left evidence of this when he drew dotted lines into a pupil's copy of the *Nocturnes* to show which notes were to coincide, as in the following[1] –

Chopin, *Nocturne*, Op.37 No.1

Lento sostenuto

[1]Quoted by Howard Ferguson in his *Keyboard Interpretation* (Oxford University Press, London 1975) p.127.

But although the method he revealed here can be regarded as broadly typical of music written by composers of his generation, it can no more be asserted as a hard-and-fast rule that all grace notes in the early 19th century should be played on the beat than that all grace notes later in the century should be played before the beat. There can be little doubt, for example, that in this familiar piece by Chopin's contemporary, Mendelssohn, the grace notes in every case come before the beat –

Allegretto grazioso   Mendelssohn, *Song without Words*, Op.62 No.6

12/1b The trill (shake)

The letters 'tr' above a note ($\overset{tr}{\rho}$), sometimes followed by a wavy line ($\overset{tr\cdots}{\rho}\rule{1cm}{0.4pt}$), indicate a **trill** (also called a 'shake'). The note is performed in rapid alternation with the note above it – . Very often, the trill is ended by a formula in which the last repetition of the principal note is preceded by the note *below* it. This can be shown by the addition of grace notes: e.g. and might be played

and . However, the absence of grace notes does not imply that the end-formula may not be used.

The number of alternations depends upon the tempo: clearly, the quicker the speed, the fewer the notes which can be fitted in. Thus

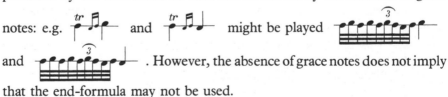

might be played at a moderate speed, or at a quick speed, or just or at a very fast one. But there is room for a good deal of flexibility, and it is often inappropriate to the character of the music to play a trill in a way which sounds mechanically regular.

Trills in music written since about the second quarter of the 19th century normally start on the written note, as in the above examples. But a trill may have to start on the upper note if it is immediately preceded by a quick statement of the written note itself. For example, 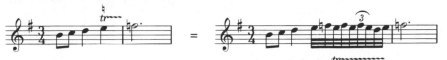 might be performed because a start on the written note would produce a quick repetition (at *) which would be awkward or even impossible to play.

If the upper note of a trill needs to be altered by an accidental, the accidental may be shown above the *tr* sign –

Alternatively, it can be indicated in brackets – . An accidental which is already contained in the key signature is not shown (unless there might be some doubt).

12/1c Arpeggiation

The sign ⦙ placed before a chord shows that the notes of the chord are to be played one after the other as quickly as possible, starting on the beat from the bottom note. Thus is meant to be played approximating to . A chord performed in this way is said to be 'arpeggiated' or, more simply, 'spread'. The arpeggio sign can embrace two staves –

= approximately

Occasionally, composers ask for chords to be arpeggiated *downwards* by using such signs as and to imply 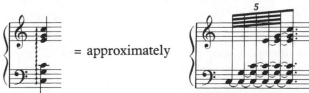 .

Grace notes are another way of showing arpeggiation – [musical notation] (see the Mendelssohn extract on p.90), but they do not have quite the same effect. Apart from the fact that after the early 19th century it became normal to play them *before* the beat, they are also not held on. Thus if the last example above were to occur at a bar-line, it would be performed approximately [musical notation] . Ties can be used, however, to show that all the notes are to be held – [musical notation] . This use of ties is exceptional, but it is clear and much less cumbersome than the 'correct' notation – [musical notation] .

12/2 Some earlier symbols

12/2a Trills (shakes) and related ornaments

In the past, trills have been indicated in many ways. During the late baroque period (e.g. in the music of J. S. Bach and his contemporaries) the most common were *tr* (sometimes written with an attached wavy line, *tr*⸺), *t*, ⌇ , ⌇ ; and these symbols continued to some extent into the early classical period (e.g. in the music of Haydn). They all tended to have the same meaning, with no distinction being made between short and long wavy lines, which in any case were often written somewhat carelessly. Unlike modern trills, they normally began on the *upper* ('auxiliary') note, although there were certain contexts in which this convention was not applied.

Context, indeed, is always a vital factor in the interpretation of these trills and shakes; and it was assumed at the time that performers would know how to exercise the necessary individual judgement. Any of the above signs might be interpreted in several different ways during the playing of a single piece of music, depending upon the length of note, the preceding and succeeding notes, its harmonic situation and even occasionally the melodic line. This is too intricate a subject to be explored in detail here, but the following points are worth noting:

(i) The alternation does not necessarily continue throughout the full value of the written note. Although *tr* is more likely to indicate a long shake and ⌇ a short shake, any of these symbols may denote either. Hence, [musical notation] , [musical notation] , [musical notation] and [musical notation] could all mean [musical notation] but might also mean [musical notation] (or [musical notation] etc.).

(ii) The termination of a long shake is rarely indicated. Sometimes the end-formula, mentioned in 12/1b, should be employed; but at other times the shake may stop on the main note without the addition of closing notes.

(iii) Other symbols were sometimes attached to the beginning or end of a wavy line to show decorated starts or finishes to a trill, but after the baroque period these were gradually superseded by grace notes (e.g. ⟋ became ⟋ and ⟋ became ⟋) – or were even written out in full.

(iv) Particularly in slow, lyrical music, shakes may sometimes be played more slowly and deliberately than would be the custom in modern usage.

(v) The signs *tr* , ∿ etc. might in some circumstances imply only a single alternation, beginning on the written note – e.g. when the written note is preceded by the same note in a lively piece of music. In his book on *Bach's Ornaments*, Walter Emery suggested the following interpretation of the opening theme of the last movement of J. S. Bach's 2nd Brandenburg Concerto –

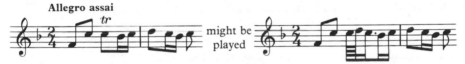

This type of short shake was called a *Schneller*.

The normal baroque practice of beginning a trill on the upper note survived well into the 19th century, but its disappearance was a gradual, not an abrupt process. Even in music of the late-18th century it cannot *invariably* be assumed that the earlier convention should still be observed.

Another type of shake in the baroque and classical periods involved the note *below* the written note. It was called a **mordent** (or *Mordant* in German), and was indicated by the symbol ∿. This could imply one or more alternations, beginning on the written note and on the beat: e.g. ⟋ is usually played ⟋ but ⟋ or ⟋ are possible in certain contexts. The symbols ∿ and ∿ were also occasionally used to specify long mordents (i.e. several alternations).

In the 19th century, ∿ and ∿ continued to be used but with a more limited application. The former came invariably to mean a single statement of the upper note (e.g. ⟋), and the latter its inversion (e.g. ⟋). Unfortunately, the names by which they were known became confused: ∿ (which was, in fact, the old *Schneller*) was sometimes called a 'mordent', and consequently ∿ (the old mordent) became an 'inverted mordent'. To prevent misunderstanding, the two are nowadays often referred to as 'upper' and 'lower' mordents respectively. Notice that an accidental required by the upper or lower note may be written above or below the ornament, e.g.

[musical notation example] = [musical notation], [musical notation] = [musical notation] (Earlier composers rarely

marked them.)

12/2b Turns

The symbol ∾ represents a melodic decoration called a **turn**. Its essential shape can best be demonstrated by a simple example: [musical notation] might be performed [musical notation] , i.e. the ornament starts on the note above the written note, then goes to the written note itself, then to the note below, and finally back to the written note. Again, any accidentals required by the upper and/or lower notes may be written above and/or below the symbol –

[musical notation] = [musical notation]

    The rhythmic interpretation of the symbol is, however, not so clear-cut. It depends upon where the ∾ is placed in the music, upon the tempo, and – to a considerable extent – upon musical feeling and taste. A distinction has to be made between a ∾ placed directly over a note and one placed between notes, e.g. between [musical notation] and [musical notation] . The former might be performed [musical notation] at a quick tempo, [musical notation] at a more moderate one, or [musical notation] at a slow tempo. If the turn is placed between two notes, it has to be thought of as a decoration leading into the second, and so it occurs just before the latter. Thus [musical notation] might be performed [musical notation] , or – at slower (and decreasing) speeds – as [musical notation] or [musical notation] etc.

At a quick tempo, or if the first note is relatively short, a turn between notes might have to be played as a group of five equal notes, e.g. [musical notation] becoming [musical notation] , but they must still be felt to lead to the following note.

A turn after a dotted note can present many possibilities, although all apply only to the dotted note itself: the rhythm of the following notes remains unchanged. Thus ♪ might be performed ♪ or ♪ or ♪ or ♪ etc., according to circumstances.

Much less common than the standard turn described above is the inverted turn. This, as its name implies, replaces the basic pattern ♪ with its inversion ♪ . The two are sometimes distinguished as 'upper' and 'lower' turns respectively. The inverted (lower) turn has been represented by various symbols, e g ↶ , ↷ and ↄ , but none of these has ever become standardised, and all are open to confusion. Moreover, Haydn frequently used ↶ to indicate an *upper* turn! Possibly to prevent misunderstandings, Haydn, Mozart and later composers sometimes indicated turns by small-size notes (e.g. ♪ instead of ♪), or even wrote out the decorations in full. During the 19th century, the use of grace notes and written-out turns became increasingly common, although some composers continued to use the symbol. In 20th-century music it is rare and can nowadays be regarded as virtually obsolete.

12/2c Appoggiaturas

The word **appoggiatura** literally means 'leaning' and refers to a note, usually dissonant, which resolves on to a weaker beat, or a weaker part of the beat, as a consonance in the same chord. In the following examples the appoggiaturas are marked * ♪ ♪ . Although there were one or two exceptions in the 18th century, it can be taken as a general rule that an appoggiatura moves to the next note above or below when it resolves.

When it is written in full-size notes (as above), there are no problems. But until about the end of the 18th century, the appoggiatura was most commonly written as a small note, with or without a slur connecting it to its resolution. The above examples could have been written ♪ and ♪ . Notice that the rhythm values of the small-size notes is ignored: the full-size notes add up to a complete bar without them.

For modern performers, the disadvantage of this method of notation is that it is not always clear just how long the appoggiatura should be – or might be – for the symbols were not rigid in their meaning. The value of the small note itself cannot be relied upon as an indication: both ♩ and ♪ ,
for example, would normally have become ♩♩ , but might also have become ♪♩ in certain circumstances. C. P. E. Bach did his best to devise a rule-of-thumb when he wrote: 'The general rule for the length of appoggiaturas is that they take half the value of the following note if it is duple and two-thirds of its length if it is triple.'[1] Thus ♩ would become
♩♩ while ♩ and ♪♩. would become ♩♩
and ♪♩♩ . C. P. E. Bach's explanation is as good a generalisation as one is likely to find, but it does not fit every situation.

For much of the 17th century, and throughout the 18th, the use of an appoggiatura was commonly assumed in certain contexts, even when none was shown. Thus ♩♩ would often have been performed ♩♩♩ . A small-size note – ♩♩ – made it plain that an appoggiatura was obligatory.

Appoggiaturas were also written as semiquavers, e.g. ♪♩♩ for ♩♩♩ .

However, during the classical period and into the 19th century there were many variations in practice concerning the use of small-size notes of short value. Mozart, for example, regularly wrote ♪, not ♪, to denote a semiquaver appoggiatura (editors generally alter his notation in this respect), though it is also likely that in certain situations he meant his ♪ signs to be interpreted in the modern way. Schumann, on the other hand, used a small-size ♪ (without the stroke) when he intended the modern ♪ . For at least the first quarter of the 19th century there was no certain distinction in notation between short, yet rhythmically measurable, appoggiaturas and notes to be played as quickly as possible. It cannot be assumed that ♪ always meant the former and ♪ the latter. Subsequently, however, the use of ♪ was generally abandoned and ♪ became established, with the implications which the symbol continues to have today. Meanwhile, the use of small-size notes to indicate long appoggiaturas had virtually disappeared.

*　　*　　*

[1]C. P. E. Bach, *Versuch über die wahre Art das Clavier zu spielen*, 1753; translated by William J. Mitchell as *Essay on the True Art of Playing Keyboard Instruments* (Cassell, London, 2nd edition 1951).

From the brief introduction which has been given, it will be realised than an appropriate interpretation of early ornament symbols often needs specialist knowledge.[1] As was pointed out at the beginning of the chapter, this is an area where the guidance of an informed editor can be particularly valuable. Nevertheless, while there may be many wrong ways of performing an ornament, there is frequently more than one right way. Nor is it ever sufficient merely to play an ornament 'correctly'. It will certainly sound wrong – and hence *be* wrong – if it is played without conviction, if it feels awkward or uncomfortable, or if it distorts the underlying melody rather than adds to its expressiveness.

[1]For further reading: Robert Donington, *The Interpretation of Early Music* (Faber, London, rev. version 1974); Walter Emery, *Bach's Ornaments* (Novello, London 1953); Howard Ferguson, *Keyboard Interpretation* (Oxford University Press, London 1975).

CHAPTER 13

Reiterations and Repeats

Many of the ornament signs explained in Chapter 12 have the advantage of avoiding the need to write out a number of notes in full. Such labour-saving devices are not only a help to the composer, but they also make the music easier to read. They can even bring about an economy in printing, since they save space. Apart from those which we have already seen, there are a number of standard methods of economising in musical notation by simplifying the representation of:

    1) rests of more than one bar;
    2) reiterated notes;
    3) repetitions of groups and bars;
    4) repeats of whole sections of music.

13/1 Rests of more than one bar

Orchestral players, particularly brass and percussion players, frequently have nothing to play for many bars on end. It would be no help to them to write as many as 30 or 40 times, or even more: with nothing to catch the eye, they would simply get lost. The methods actually used assist comprehension as well as save space. Traditionally rests of up to eight bars had individual signs –

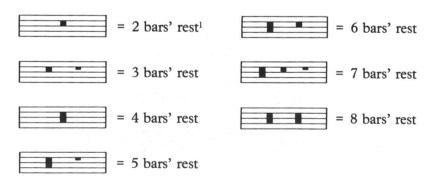

    = 2 bars' rest[1]   = 6 bars' rest

    = 3 bars' rest   = 7 bars' rest

    = 4 bars' rest   = 8 bars' rest

    = 5 bars' rest

These symbols are now virtually obsolete, but the traditional way of showing rests of nine or more bars is still used –

[1]This is the same as the breve rest: see 3/1.

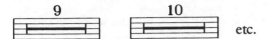 etc.

Indeed, this method is now used for *any* number of bars' rest from two upwards, although other symbols are also used for this purpose –

13/2 Reiterated notes

No explanation of these shorthand devices is needed apart from their written-out equivalents –

Further subdivisions are indicated by additional strokes; thus three strokes – etc. – represent demisemiquaver reiterations.

Patterns of alternating notes can be shown similarly –

¹It should be noted, however, that the same signs were originally used as ornament signs, e.g. in English and Dutch keyboard music of the late 16th–17th centuries, when two strokes through a stem, or above or below a note, were commonly used to indicate a shake.

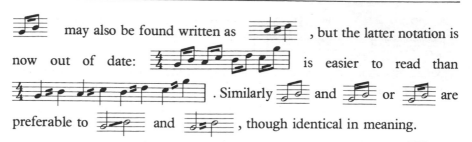 may also be found written as [notation], but the latter notation is now out of date: [notation] is easier to read than [notation]. Similarly [notation] and [notation] or [notation] are preferable to [notation] and [notation], though identical in meaning.

More rapid alternations can be shown by the same method: [notation] and [notation], for example, mean alternations of $\flat$ s. However, if very short time values are used or if the tempo is very fast, all that may be intended is that the alternation of the notes should be as quick as possible, i.e. not strictly counted. Careful composers add the word *tremolo* (or *trem.*) when they want this effect.

13/3 Repetitions of groups and bars

When a chord is repeated exactly on every beat in a bar, the repetitions do not always have to be written out in full –

may be written

Repetitions of quaver groups may also be shown by the same oblique stroke between the second and fourth lines of the stave –

may be written

but repetitions of semiquaver groups require two strokes –

and demisemiquaver groups three strokes –

Groups consisting of a mixture of rhythmic values may be shown by two oblique strokes with dots either side –

and a complete bar, which can be repeated as often as necessary, by a single oblique stroke with dots either side –

The repetition of a short passage – rarely more than two or three bars – may be shown by the word *bis* (twice) in the middle of a square bracket above it –

may be written as –

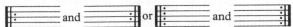

13/4 Repeats of whole sections of music

There is another way of showing that a passage is to be repeated: by placing dots (either two or four) in the spaces of the stave inside a double bar-line at the beginning and end of the section to be repeated –

and

or

and

(In the following examples two dots, which are more customary, will be used for repeat signs, but four dots could be substituted in each case.)

If the passage to be repeated occurs at the very beginning of a piece, the first set of dots is omitted. At the first repeat sign in a piece, therefore, one repeats from the beginning, but at all others one goes back to the previous repeat sign. Thus

is to be performed

A repeat direction can be placed at any point in a bar, not just at the end. When it occurs in the middle of a bar, however, the time values must be so arranged that the bars would be complete if the passage were written out in full. Thus

is to be performed

(The two notes marked * are not *dotted* crotchets, because the sixth quaver of the bar is provided in the repeat.)

The end of a passage which is repeated can be altered when it is played the second time by the use of ⌐1⌐ and ⌐2⌐ directions. These mean 'first time' and 'second time'. Thus

is to be performed

The first- and second-time directions can embrace more than one bar, as in the next example – which also shows (underneath) how bars are numbered for reference. Notice in bar *3b* that the ⌐2 is unclosed at the end since it leads into fresh music; the repeat dots at this point show that the following section will also be repeated.

Although the repeated passages in the above examples are all very short, much longer repeats – often of several pages – are also common.

There are two other standard directions for repeating sections of music which have already been performed. The first is the instruction **Da Capo**, often abbreviated as **D.C.**, meaning 'from the beginning': i.e. the performer is to start again at the beginning of the written music. The place to finish is then shown by the word **Fine** (Italian for 'end'), or by a ⌒ (not observed the first time round), or by both together.

A similar instruction is **Dal Segno**, or **D.S.** for short, meaning 'from the sign'. The sign in question is shown 𝄋 or :𝄋: , so the performer returns to this point and plays on again until he comes to the word *Fine* and/or ⌒.

Sometimes the instructions are written out more fully but with the same meaning: *Da Capo al Fine* (repeat from the beginning as far as *Fine*); *Dal Segno al Fine* (repeat from the sign as far as *Fine*). However, more complicated instructions are also to be found, usually involving the phrase '*e poi*' which means 'and then', e.g. *D.C. al Segno e poi la Coda* (repeat from the beginning as far as the sign, and then play the coda).

In practice, composers' instructions about repeats are not always observed. Generalisations about whether or not this is justified are dangerous, but there may sometimes be a case for ignoring a repeat sign shown by dots. One place where it is even customary to do so occurs when a section is played again following a *D.C.* or a *D.S.* instruction, as, for example in the repetition of the Minuet after the Trio in the classical minuet-and-trio form (e.g. in the symphonies of Haydn and Mozart). To ignore a *D.C.* or a *D.S.* instruction itself, however, usually upsets the balance of the music as a whole. Indeed, the two directions often occur on chords other than the tonic, where the music *cannot* stop but must continue until it reaches the end as shown by *Fine* etc.

APPENDIX A

Irregular Divisions of Compound Time Values

As the information in 5/5b implies, two different methods of writing irregular divisions of compound time values are used. Both are likely to be encountered – sometimes in the course of a single piece! The essence of the matter may be summarised thus –

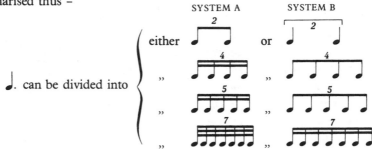

Like groups of 7, irregular groups of 8–11 would be written as ♪ s in System A and as ♪ s in System B. Irregular groups of 13–23 would then have to be written as ♪ s in System A and as ♪ s in System B.

Divisions of other compound units can be obtained by adjusting the time values in the above table, for example –

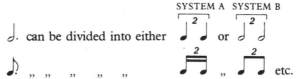

As outlined above, each system is consistent within itself. (In System A the time taken by each irregular group would always be shorter if the figure were removed; in System B it would always be longer.) Confusion can be avoided by sticking to one system or the other, and not mixing the two. Thus –

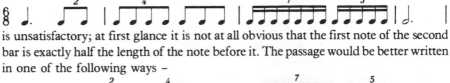

is unsatisfactory; at first glance it is not at all obvious that the first note of the second bar is exactly half the length of the note before it. The passage would be better written in one of the following ways –

Logic, it may be thought, is clearly on the side of System A, although in practice composers often use it only for duplets, all other irregular groups being written in System B. Fortunately, what is intended is usually clear because it can be deduced from the time signature and the remaining notes in the bar.

APPENDIX B

Notes and Keys in English, German, French, Italian

English	German	French	Italian
C	C	Ut	Do
C sharp	Cis	Ut dièse	Do diesis
C flat	Ces	Ut bémol	Do bemolle
D	D	Ré	Re
D sharp	Dis	Ré dièse	Re diesis
D flat	Des	Ré bémol	Re bemolle
E	E	Mi	Mi
E sharp	Eis	Mi dièse	Mi diesis
E flat	Es	Mi bémol	Mi bemolle
F	F	Fa	Fa
F sharp	Fis	Fa dièse	Fa diesis
F flat	Fes	Fa bémol	Fa bemolle
G	G	Sol	Sol
G sharp	Gis	Sol dièse	Sol diesis
G flat	Ges	Sol bémol	Sol bemolle
A	A	La	La
A sharp	Ais	La dièse	La diesis
A flat	As	La bémol	La bemolle
B	H*	Si	Si
B sharp	His	Si dièse	Si diesis
B flat	B*	Si bémol	Si bemolle
major	Dur	majeur	maggiore
minor	Moll	mineur	minore
sharp	Kreuz	dièse	diesis
double sharp	Doppelkreuz	double dièse	doppio diesis
flat	Be	bémol	bemolle
double flat	Doppel-Be	double bémol	doppio bemolle
natural	Auflösungszeichen or Quadrat	bécarre	bequadro

*Note that in German ♭o is called B and ♮o is H. Thus it is possible to write BACH in musical notes: ♭o o o ♮o

GLOSSARY

Foreign Words used for Performance Directions

(Abbreviations: I = Italian, L = Latin, F = French, G = German, lit. = literally)

a (I), **à** (F)   at, to, by, for, in, in the style of
aber (G)   but
a cappella (I)   unaccompanied (referring to choral music – lit. 'in church style')
accelerando, accel. (I)   gradually getting faster
adagietto (I)   rather slow, but faster than *adagio*
adagio (I)   slow (lit. 'at ease'), generally held to indicate a tempo between *andante* and *largo*
à deux, à 2 (F), **a due, a 2** (I)   for two performers or instruments (in orchestral or band music, it means that a part is to be played in unison by two instruments)
ad libitum, ad lib. (L)   at choice, meaning either that a passage may be performed freely or that an instrument in a score may be omitted
affettuoso (I)   tenderly
affrettando, affret. (I)   hurrying
agitato (I)   agitated
al, alla (I)   to the, in the manner of
à la pointe (F)   use the bow (of a string instrument) at the point, i.e. the end opposite to that held by the player
alla breve (I)   with a minim beat, equivalent to $\frac{2}{2}$ (C); i.e. implying a faster tempo than the notes might otherwise suggest (see 1/2)
alla marcia (I)   in the style of a march
allargando (I)   broadening, i.e. getting a little slower and probably also a little louder
allegretto (I)   fairly quick, but not quite as quick as *allegro*
allegro (I)   quick (lit. 'cheerful')
als (G)   than
alt (I)   high (*in alt* is used in vocal music to refer to notes in the octave above the treble stave, starting with the G; *in altissimo*, in the octave above that)
al tallone (I)   see *au talon*
amabile (I)   amiable, pleasant
am Frosch (G)   see *au talon*
amore (I), **amour** (F)   love
amoroso (I)   loving
andante (I)   at a walking pace (lit. 'going'), indicating a medium speed (*più andante* and *molto andante* are somewhat slower)
andantino (I)   slightly faster than *andante* (but it can also mean slightly slower: the term is ambiguous)

an der Spitze (G)   see *à la pointe*

anima (I)   soul, spirit (*con anima* is ambiguous, meaning either 'with feeling' or 'spirited')

animando (I)   becoming more lively

animato (I), **animé** (F)   animated, lively

apaisé (F)   calmed

a piacere (I)   at pleasure, meaning that the performer is not bound to follow the given rhythm exactly

appassionato (I)   with passion

a punto d'arco (I)   see *à la pointe*

arco (I)   bow of a string instrument, a direction after *pizzicato* (see 19/2)

assai (I)   very, extremely (but sometimes used in the same sense as *assez*)

assez (F)   enough, sufficiently (but sometimes used in the same sense as *assai*)

a tempo (I)   in time, indicating a return to the original speed after e.g. *rit.*, *rall.*

attacca (I)   go straight on, indicating an immediate move to the next section of music

Ausdruck (G)   expression (*ausdrucksvoll*: expressively)

au talon (F)   use the bow (of a string instrument) at the heel, i.e. the end held by the player

avec (F)   with

ben, bene (I)   well, very

bestimmt (G)   with decision, definite

bewegt (G)   with movement, agitated

bis (I)   twice, indicating the repetition of a short passage (see 13/3)

bravura (I)   skill, brilliance (*con bravura*: in a brilliant style)

breit (G)   broad, expansive

brillante (I), **brillant** (F)   brilliant

brio (I)   vigour, animation (*brioso, con brio*: with vigour)

calando (I)   getting softer, dying away (and usually slowing down)

calmato (I), **calme** (F)   calm, tranquil

cantabile (I)   in a singing style

cantando (I)   singing

capriccioso (I), **capricieux** (F)   in a whimsical, fanciful style

cédez (F)   yield, relax the speed

col, coll', colla, colle (I)   with, with the

colla parte (I)   keep with the soloist, a direction to an accompanist

colla voce (I)   keep with the singer, a direction to an accompanist

col legno (I)   with the wood, a direction to a string player to play with the wood of the bow rather than with the hair (see 19/2)

coll' ottava (I)   with the octave, a direction to a keyboard player to double notes an octave higher, or lower if *bassa* is added

come (I), **comme** (F)   as, similar to

come prima (I)   as before (not necessarily as at the beginning)

come sopra (I)   as above (= *come prima*)

comodo (I)   convenient (*tempo comodo*: at a comfortable speed)

con (I)   with
corda, corde (I)   string, strings (see *una corda, tre corde*)
crescendo, cresc., cres. (I)   gradually getting louder

da (I)   from
da capo, D.C. (I)   from the beginning (see 13/4)
dal segno, D.S. (I)   from the sign (see 13/4)
Dämpfer (G)   mute
deciso (I)   with determination
decrescendo, decresc., decres. (I)   gradually getting softer
delicato (I)   delicate
détaché (F)   detached, usually applying to bowing on string instruments
diminuendo, dimin., dim. (I)   gradually getting softer
divisi, div. (I)   divided, a direction to orchestral players (usually strings) to divide
     into two or more groups (see 22/2)
doch (G)   however, yet
dolce (I)   sweet, soft (*dolcissimo, dolciss.*: as sweetly as possible)
dolente (I)   sad, mournful
dolore (I)   grief (*doloroso*: sorrowful)
doppio movimento (I)   twice as fast
douce, doux (F)   soft, sweet (*doucement*: softly, sweetly)
duolo (I)   = *dolore*

e, ed (I)   and
égal (F), **eguale** (I)   equal
ein (G)   a
einfach (G)   simple
Empfindung (G)   emotion, feeling (*empfindungsvoll*: with feeling)
emporté (F)   fiery, impetuous
en animant (F)   becoming more lively
en cédant (F)   yielding
en dehors (F)   prominent (lit. 'outside'), a direction to make a melody stand out
energico (I)   energetic
enlevez (F)   take up, take off, a direction for a pedal or a mute
en mesure (F)   in time
en pressant (F)   hurrying on
en retenant (F)   holding back (slowing a little)
en serrant (F)   becoming quicker
espressione (I)   expression
espressivo, espress., espr. (I), **expressif** (F)   expressive
estinto (I)   as soft as possible, lifeless
et (F)   and
etwas (G)   somewhat, rather

f   see *forte*
facile (I, F)   easy
felice (I)   happy

feroce (I)   fierce
feurig (G)   fiery
fin (F), **fine** (I)   end
Flatterzunge, Flzg. (G)   flutter-tonguing, a direction for wind instruments (see 20/6)
flautato, flautando (I)   flute-like, a direction for natural harmonics on string instruments (see 19/4)
flessibile (I)   flexible, i.e. not in strict tempo
fliessend (G)   flowing
flottant (F)   floating
forte, f (I)   loud (*fortissimo, ff, fff*: very loud – see 10/2)
fortepiano, fp (I)   loud, then immediately soft
forza (I)   force (*forzando, forzato, fz*: forcing, strongly accenting)
frei (G)   free
fretta (I)   haste
frisch (G)   vigorous
fröhlich (G)   cheerful, joyful
fuoco (I)   fire
furioso (I)   furious, frenzied

gebunden (G)   joined
gehend (G)   at a steady speed (lit. 'going'), equivalent to *andante*
gesangvoll (G)   in a singing style, equivalent to *cantabile*
geschwind (G)   quick
giocoso (I)   playful, humorous
giojoso (I)   joyful, merry
giusto (I)   proper, exact (*tempo giusto*: in strict time)
glissando, gliss. (pseudo-I)   slide (a rapid scale passage produced by e.g. drawing a thumb or finger-tip along the white keys of a piano, or by sweeping the fingers across the strings of a harp see – 19/7 – or by sliding the finger along a string of string instrument
G.P. (G – *Generalpause*)   an indication to individual performers that *all* are silent (see 10/1)
gracieux (F)   graceful
grandioso (I)   grandly
grave (I, F)   very slow, solemn
grazioso (I)   graceful

immer (G)   always
impetuoso (I)   impetuous
incalzando (I)   getting quicker (lit. 'pressing forward')
innig (G)   heartfelt, sincere
inquieto (I)   restless
in relievo (I)   prominent (lit. 'in relief'), a direction to make a melody stand out

joyeux (F)   joyful

kräftig (G)   strong

lacrimoso, lagrimando, lagrimoso (I)   sad (lit. 'tearful')

lamentoso (I)   lamenting

langsam (G)   slow, equivalent to *adagio* and *lento*

largamente (I)   broadly

larghetto (I)   rather slow, but slightly faster than *largo*

largo (I)   slow, stately

lebhaft (G)   lively, equivalent to *vivace*

legato (I)   smooth (lit. 'bound', 'tied'), indicating no break between notes
  (*legatissimo*: as smooth as possible)

légèrement (F), **leggiero** (I), **leicht** (G)   light, nimble

Leid (G)   grief, pain (*leidvoll, leidensvoll*: sorrowful)

Leidenschaft (G)   passion (*leidenschaftlich*: passionate)

leise (G)   soft, gentle

lent (F), **lento** (I)   slow (*lentement*: slowly)

liberamente (I), **librement** (F)   freely

licenza (I)   licence, freedom (*con alcuna licenza*: with some freedom, particularly
  with regard to tempo and rhythm)

lieblich (G)   lovely

l'istesso (I)   the same (*l'istesso tempo*: at the same speed)

loco (I)   at the normal pitch (used to cancel an 8va direction – see 2/1 – or to
  confirm that one is not intended)

lointain (F), **lontano** (I)   distant

lourd (F)   heavy, equivalent to *pesante*

lugubre (I)   mournful

lunga (I)   long (*lunga pausa*: long pause – see 10/1)

lusingando (I)   coaxing; in a sweet, persuasive style

lustig (G)   cheerful

m   see *main, mano, mezza*

ma (I)   but (e.g. *allegro ma non troppo*: quick but not too quick)

maestoso (I)   majestic

main (F)   hand (*main gauche, m.g.*: left hand; *main droite, m.d.*: right hand)

mais (F)   but

mano (I)   hand (*mano sinistra, m.s.*: left hand; *mano destra, m.d.*: right hand)

mancando (I)   fading away

marcato, marc. (I)   emphatic, accented

martelé (F), **martellato** (I)   strongly accented (lit. 'hammered'), generally used
  in string music to denote a particular type of bowing, but can also be applied to
  music for piano or other instruments

marziale (I)   in a military style

mässig (G)   at a moderate speed

meno (I)   less

mesto (I)   sad

mezza, mezzo (I)   half (*mezzo forte, mf*: moderately loud; *mezzo piano, mp*:
  moderately soft; *mezza voce*: in an undertone)

misterioso (I)   mysterious

misura (I)   measure (*alla misura*: in strict time; *senza misura*: in free time)

mit (G)   with

moderato (I), **modéré** (F)   at a moderate speed

moins (F)   less

molto (I)   very, much

morendo (I)   dying away

mosso (I)   with motion, animated

moto, movimento (I)   movement, motion

mouvement, mouvt (F)   movement, motion (*au mouvement*: in time; *premier (1er) mouvement*: original tempo)

munter (G)   lively

muta (I)   change, e.g. as in changing the tuning of a kettle drum or in transferring from one instrument to another

nach und nach (G)   gradually

naturale, nat. (I)   in the ordinary way, a direction to a singer or instrumentalist to resume the normal method of performance (e.g. after a *col legno* passage in string music)

nicht (G)   not

niente (I)   nothing

nobilmente (I)   nobly

noch (G)   still, yet

non (I, F)   not

nuovo (I)   new (*di nuovo*: again)

obbligato (I)   obligatory, indicating that an instrument has a special role and is essential (though the word is sometimes incorrectly used to mean 'optional')

ohne (G)   without

ossia (I)   or, alternatively (often used to indicate a simpler version of a difficult passage)

ostinato (I)   persistent, generally referring to a persistently repeated rhythm or melodic figure (a *basso ostinato* is a bass line with this feature)

ottava, ott. (I)   octave (*ottava bassa*: octave lower; *ottava alta*: octave higher)

p   see *piano*

parlando (I)   speaking, a direction to sing in a conversational style

patetico (I)   with deep feeling, with pathos (*not* 'pathetic' in the sense of feeble!)

pausa (I)   a pause

pedale (I), **pédale** (F)   pedal

per (I)   by, for, through, to

perdendosi (I)   dying away

pesante (I)   heavy

peu (F)   little (*peu à peu*: little by little, gradually)

piacevole (I)   pleasant

piangevole (I)   plaintive, in the style of a lament

piano, p (I)   quiet (*pianissimo, pp, ppp*: very quiet)

pietoso, pietosamente (I)   tenderly (lit. 'pitifully')

più (I)   more

pizzicato, pizz. (I)   plucked, a direction for plucking the strings of a bowed instrument (see 19/2)

placido (I)   calm, peaceful

plus (F)   more

pochettino, poch. (I)   rather little

pochissimo, pochiss. (I)   very little

poco (I)   little, slightly (*poco a poco*: little by little, gradually)

poi (I)   then

ponticello (I)   bridge (on a string instrument)

portamento (I)   slide from one note to the next (lit. 'carrying'), a direction to a voice, bowed instrument or trombone (but not to keyboard instruments since they always play in 'steps' of at least a semitone)

possibile (I)   possible (e.g. *presto possibile*: as fast as possible)

precipitando, precipitato, precipitoso (I)   rushing, headlong

presser, pressez (F)   hurry

presto (I)   fast, a tempo faster than *allegro* (*prestissimo*: very fast)

prima, primo (I)   first (*prima volta*: first time, used to distinguish between two different interpretations of a repeated section of music; *tempo primo*, first speed, used to revert to the opening tempo of a piece of music)

quasi (I, L)   as if, resembling (e.g. *quasi recitativo*: like a recitative)

ralentir (F)   slacken, slow down

rallentando, rall. (I)   gradually getting slower (see 10/1)

rasch (G)   quick (*rascher*: quicker)

repetizione, replica (I)   repetition

retenu (F)   held back, i.e. a little slower

rigoroso (I)   strict

rinforzando, rinforzato, rinf., rfz, rf (I)   reinforcing (see 10/2)

risoluto (I)   bold, strong

ritardando, ritard., rit. (I)   gradually getting slower (see 10/1)

ritenuto, riten., rit. (I)   held back (see 10/1)

ritmico (I)   rhythmically

rubato, tempo rubato (I)   with some freedom of time (lit. 'robbed' – see 10/1)

ruhig (G)   peaceful

saltando, saltato (I)   see *sautillé*

sans (F)   without

sautillé (F)   springing, a lightly bouncing bow technique on string instruments

scherzando, scherzoso (I)   playful, joking (*scherzo*: a joke; implies a fast speed)

schleppen, schleppend (G)   dragging

schnell (G)   fast (*schneller*: faster)

schwach (G)   weak (*schwächer*: weaker)

sec (F), **secco** (I)   crisp (lit. 'dry'), suppress the sound as quickly as possible – do not allow it to continue to reverberate (see 19/2c)

seconda, secondo (I) second (*seconda volta*: second time)

segue (I) go straight on (lit. 'follow')

sehr (G) very

semplice (I) simple, plain

sempre (I) always

senza (I) without (e.g. *senza rigore*: freely, lit. 'without strictness')

seul (F) alone

serrer, serrez (F) hurry, quicken, equivalent to *stringendo*

sforzando, sforzato, sfz, sf (I) accented, forced (see 10/2)

simile, sim. (I) continue in the same way

sino, sin' (I) until, up to (*sin' al fine*: until the end)

slargando, slentando (I) getting slower

slancio (I) enthusiasm, impetus (*con slancio*: with impetuosity)

smorzando, smorz. (I) dying away in tone and speed

soave (I) gentle, smooth

solenne (I) solemn, grave

sonoramente (I), **sonore** (F), **sonoro** (I) resonant, with rich tone

sopra (I) above, on, e.g. a direction for keyboard players to place one hand over the other (see also *come sopra*)

sordino, sord. (I) mute (*con sordini*: with mutes; *senza sordini*: without mutes – see 19/2, 20/5 and 21/3b)

sospirando (I) sighing

sostenuto, sost. (I) sustained

sotto (I) below, e.g. a direction for keyboard players to place one hand below the other

sotto voce (I) in an undertone (lit. 'below the voice')

sourdine (F) mute

sous (F) under

spiccato (I) detached (lit. 'clearly articulated') a bouncing bow techique on string instruments

spiritoso (I) spirited

staccato, stacc. (I) detached, short (see 11/3) (*staccatissimo*: very short)

stark (G) strong

strepitoso (I) noisy, boisterous

stretto (I) quickening the speed (also means overlapping entries of a fugue subject)

stringendo (I) gradually getting faster

subito, sub. (I) suddenly

sul, sulla (I) on the (e.g. *sul G*: on the G string; *sul ponticello*: near (lit. 'on') the bridge – see 19/2)

süss (G) sweet

tacet (L) silent, a direction that a particular part has nothing to play in a section of music

tanto (I) so much

tasto (I)   the fingerboard of a string instrument (*sul tasto*: on the fingerboard) or the key of a keyboard (*tasto solo*, *T.S.*: a direction to a continuo player not to add anything above the given bass)

tempo (I)   speed (*a tempo*: in time)

teneramente (I)   tenderly

tenerezza (I)   tenderness

tenuto, ten. (I)   held (see 11/3)

tosto (I)   swift, rapid (but often used in the same sense as *troppo*)

tranquillo (I)   calm

traurig (G)   sad

tre (I)   three (*tre corde*: three strings, a direction to pianists to release the left pedal – see 21/3b)

tremolando, tremolo, trem. (I)   trembling, a direction for the rapid reiterations of a single note or alternations of different notes (see 13/2, 19/2)

très (F)   very

trionfale (I)   triumphant

tristamente (I), **triste** (I, F)   sad

troppo (I)   too much

tutti (I)   all, everyone

un (F), **una, uno** (I)   one (*una corda*: one string, a direction for pianists to press the left pedal – see 21/3b)

und (G)   and

unisono, unis. (I)   in unison, with everyone performing the same notes, a direction to cancel *divisi*

veloce (I)   swift

vibrato (I)   vibrating (see 19/5)

viel (G)   much

vif (F)   lively

vigoroso (I)   vigorous, strong

vite (F)   quick

vivace (I), **vivement** (F), **vivo** (I)   lively, quick

voce (I), **voix** (F)   voice (*mezza voce*: in an undertone, softly)

volante (I)   flying, fast

voll (G)   full

volta (I)   time (*prima volta*: first time)

volti subito, V.S. (I)   turn (the page) at once

vorgetragen (G)   brought out, prominent

wenig (G)   little

wieder (G)   again

zart (G)   tender, delicate

ziemlich (G)   moderately

zu (G)   to, too

INDEX